Underground

delicacies

for the

quick-crunch,

virtual reality,

Zen-soaked,

blaster

nineties.

giga bites

THE HACKER COOKBOOK
by JENZ JOHNSON

TEN SPEED PRESS
BERKELEY, CA

Giga Bites: The Hacker Cookbook

A KIRSTY MELVILLE BOOK

TEN SPEED PRESS
P.O. Box 7123
Berkeley, CA 94707

Cover and text design by Big Fish Books, San Francisco

Library of Congress Cataloging-in-Publication Data
Johnson, Jenz.
      Giga bites: the hacker cookbook / by Jenz Johnson.
      p. cm.
      ISBN 0-89815-644-0
      1. Cookery—Humor. 2. Computers—Humor. I. Title.
      PN6231.C624J57 1994
614.5'0207—dc20   94-16297
                       CIP

FIRST PRINTING 1994
Printed in the United States of America by Malloy Lithographing, Inc.
1 2 3 4 5 6 7 8 9 10

Contents

....

Acknowledgements

Apple is a registered trademark of Apple Computer, Inc.; Baby Ruth and Butterfinger are registered trademarks of The Nestlé Corporation; Betty Crocker is a registered trademark of General Mills, Inc.; Brillo is a registered trademark of American National Can; Campbell's and Spaghettios are registered trademarks of the Campbell Soup Company; Cheetos is a registered trademark of Frito-Lay, Inc.; Cheez Whiz, Velveeta, Kool-Aid and Jell-O are registered trademarks of Kraft General Foods, Inc.; Coke is a registered trademark of The Coca-Cola Company; Cool Whip is a trademark of Kraft General Foods, Inc.; Ex-Lax is a registered trademark of Sandoz Pharmaceuticals Corporation; 409 is a registered trademark of the Clorox Company; Galloping Gourmet is a registered trademark of Wilbur Freifeld; Heath and Milk Duds are registered trademarks of Leaf, Inc.; Jolt is a registered trademark of the Jolt Company, Inc.; M&Ms and Snickers are registered trademarks of Mars, Inc.; Mountain Dew is a registered trademark of PepsiCo, Inc.; Newman's Own is a registered trademark of Newman's Own, Inc.; Nintendo is a registered trademark of Nintendo Entertainment Systems; NoDoz is a registered trademark of Bristol Myers Squibb Co.; Oreos and Ritz are registered trademarks of Nabisco, Inc.; Pentium is a trademark of Intel Corporation; PopTarts is a registered trademark of the Kellogg Company; Porsche is a registered trademark of Porsche Inter-Auto GMBH; PowerPC is a trademark of IBM Corporation; Reese's Pieces is a registered trademark of Hershey Foods, Inc.; Ronco is a registered trademark of Ronco Corporation; The Salvation Army is a regstered trademark of The Salvation Army; Sega and Genesis are registered trademarks of SEGA; Shamu is a registered trademark of Sea World, Inc.; Slim Jims is a registered trademark of General Mills, Inc.; Spam is a registered trademark of Geo. A. Hormel & Company; SPARC is a registered trademark of Sun Microsystems, Inc.; Tabasco is a registered trademark of McIlhenny Company; Teflon is a registered trademark of E.I. DuPont De Nemours and Company; Twinkies and Wonder are registered trademarks of Continental Baking Company; Veg-O-Matic is a registered trademark of Popeil Brothers, Inc.; Vitalis is a registered trademark of Clairol, Inc.

Preface

THE IDEA FOR this book came early one morning when I found myself channel surfing. The only good program on cable was Ronco's new infomercial about his miracle bald-spot remover. It is magic: one spray with his colored powder, and bald spots disappear. It is the Veg-O-Matic of the nineties.

There is this wonderful part when Ronco sprays the top of one man's head. Bingo, no more bald spot. Ronco turns to the man's wife, standing right by him, and asks, "What do you think?" She bursts into a big, bright smile. The years melt away; they are young again and in love. "He's beautiful," she says.

The man turns, and they share the moment.

This is one of the few spontaneous spots left on early morning cable. I always stop what I am eating to experience the happiness of their reclaimed youth.

This particular morning a friend rings up unexpectedly. "You awake?" she asks.

I am sitting quarter-lotus position on my couch (which also serves as my bed). It is after 2:00, and except for the chrome reflection from my bicycle, I am alone in the pitch black, TV blazing.

"Still hacking?" she asks.

"Nah," I say.

I look down at my hands and find that I have whipped together a great snack: a can of refried beans, a jar of Cheez Whiz, some green chilies, and some leftover Chinese food, all stirred together in a large bowl. And I am scooping the stuff out with beef jerky sticks. It is a mighty tasty combination, the perfect accompaniment to cable.

She replies, "That sounds great. I've got a bad case of the munchies myself." For a nanosecond, I pause. It is a revelation. Even in our darkest, most private moments, my digital generation is connected, our stomachs grinding to a common beat. I flash on the meals I've loved: the dips, the whiz concoctions, ones I've eaten too fast to remember,

5

ones that came back on the spoon, or others that I confess were simply flashes in the pan.

"Come on over," I say. "There's plenty."

I know there won't be much time for sleep tonight, so this is no different than my hacking nights. But I begin to think about the hacker's special blend of food. If we ever stop our maddening pace and look down at our spontaneous dinners, we will find ourselves elbow deep in some of the most provocative inventions since our own programming.

This book is the result of a lot of personal gorging. Collected on these pages are myriad recipes, improvised during and between bouts of computer hacking.

Leave your preconceptions at the door and enjoy.

—jj

Introduction

The Elements of Hacker Style

THIS BOOK CELEBRATES hackers and their favorite foods. The recipes in this book have evolved or spontaneously erupted for decades in computer labs around the country, and for hackers they require no introduction. However, for many laypeople to appreciate what goes on in a hacker's stomach may require an understanding of what goes on in that hacker's mind.

This chapter introduces the hacker mind and its innate connection to his stomach.

What Is a Hacker?

The hacker is simply a technology fanatic—with the emphasis on *fanatic*.

A hacker is *not* the bespectacled nerd of the fifties with a slide rule dangling from his belt, glasses askew at the end of his nose. No longer. Hackers are both male and female and are at the vanguard of the fast-growing community of knowl-edge workers. Intense, driven, they can pull sixteen-hour days producing new generations of software, special effects for movies,[1] and new machines that set our informational world on fire. Far from the fringes of society, hackers are at the epicenter, responsible in part for the continued technological advancement worldwide and for fueling the economic growth in their respective countries.

Millions of hackers are not old enough to drive: Young computer and game enthusiasts also "hack," spending hours in front of their Nintendos, Sega Genesis machines, or Apple computers. It is estimated that over 70 percent of homes with a child between the ages of eight and twelve have a Nintendo game set.

Hackers love computers—the pitter-patter of hard disk accesses, the smell of the ozone, the

---

[1] *Jurassic Park* is one current example of hacker work.

jumble of code that comprises the operating system. To a hacker, the computer is a source of pure beauty and fascination—a perfected state of intelligence embodied in a machine. Years of refinement have transformed the monolithic card-reading, batch-processing clunkers of decades past into the svelte SPARC-, Pentium- and PowerPC-supercharged desktop workhorses. These are truly the Porsches of the computer world. And hackers can spend their entire waking hours in front of a machine coding fresh nuances or exploring the vast reaches of network life beyond their keyboards.

This work is a life-affirming activity for most hackers, a stimulating and challenging way to spend their time. In fact, for most hackers, physical reality ceases to have relevance the farther they are from their computers.[2]

Hacking

To understand a hacker, you must first understand the nature of hacking. Given the great lusting between hackers and their machines, hacking is the Act. It is the continual and unstoppable refinement of technical minutiae—not all that different from assembling a model airplane or completing a needlepoint, except that the tools are a program-

ming language or a set of circuit boards. The hacker refines a portion of a computer program or a hardware design until the resulting technology is pure lightning.

Take a simple example of the hacker who wants to equip his machine with computer shorthand. He wants to type a short abbreviation like "cy" and have the computer automatically expand it to "cybernetics."

To do this, the hacker finds the seams in the operating system—those junctures where one module in the operating system hands control over to another. The hacker finds how the user's keystrokes are temporarily stored, then inserts a routine that first searches for abbreviations and expands them to their equivalents. In this work, each movement of information into and out of registers is carefully choreographed. Invariably the hacker will notice bugs[3] where the routine simply failed—either it choked or gagged or bounced or crashed. The hacker corrects these then refines his code, pushing for performance, eliminating superfluous computer statements. The end result is a convenient feature that can be loaded into his machine every time it is turned on. He can place his routine out on the network for others to use and refine.

While hacking, he must keep various parts of

---

[2]In general, relevance is directly proportional to the exponential distance between a hacker and his screen (Klimmer's axiom).

[3] Errors that cause the machine to malfunction or produce faulty results.

the computer's processes in his mind. He must recall the various steps and variables that he has assigned to keep information. At the same time, he must work quickly and efficiently so as to keep this picture and its ultimate solution vividly in mind. He will work through a series of precise logical steps that take raw input (in this example, the keystrokes) and produce a highly refined end product.

One false step—a misspelling, a misplaced comma, or inconsistent type—will be disastrous and may lead to weeks of debugging.[4]

So hackers must operate in an intense, focused world sometimes referred to as *cyberspace* or *hyperspace*. They maintain a mind-set that tolerates few interruptions because of their possible impact on the precision of the code. As the hacker is careening through his world, sometimes for weeks or months on end, he enters an all-consuming reality—a reality more engaging, more rewarding, than his physical space. This is his cyberspace, where he wants to live forever.

The Hacker Creed

In this world of intense precision, the hacker is pitted against the computer itself. Not that the computer is infallible—it is after all a machine that can run out of paper and refuse even to start when a minor mishap occurs. However, the computer is absolute. It behaves precisely the way its designers have dictated. As a hacker goes about his daily business of nudging the machine more toward his image, the computer leaves its indelible footprint, a sliver of microcode that lodges in hacker synapses. The result is that the hacker tries to emulate the machine.

This mind-set becomes the springboard for the hacker's creed—rules by which hackers live. The creed can be summarized by the following rules.

■ "Do Nothing Which Is of No Use." Culled from the writings of the famous samurai protégé Miyamoto Musashi,[5] who killed a remarkable sixty people before he was thirty years old, the saying directs that a person not be wasteful. For the hacker, nothing is more disgusting than wasting time. One should eliminate superfluous activities much the same way that one should eliminate superfluous computer code. After all, long after he is gone, the hacker will be known for the tightness of his code. Nothing else matters: not his dress, or his behaviors, or his appearance.

■ Push the Envelope. Hackers continually push the envelope of technology and, with it, the tolerances of acceptable behavior. While hacking, they consider everything else to be excess: they

---

[4] This activity, sometimes referred to as *bug busting*, is akin to delousing: The hacker plays computer and follows the instructions in the code to locate an error.

[5] See Miyamoto Musashi, *A Book of Five Rings* (Woodstock, New York: Overlook Press, 1974): 49.

keep long hours in hack mode, furiously typing and consuming large quantities of food. There are no bounds for the hacking hacker. Even physical relationships have been supplanted by the advent of high-speed networks and communications technologies. The hacker is not one to stop when he can't see bottom. He will continue to move and push all boundaries aside in his insatiable appetite to explore new realms.

■ What Is Not Private Is Free. All information should be free—unless, of course, the author deems it private. This most notably applies to the airways—the networks and on-line services—where hackers do their information surfing. Any information found here is free. To expect some sort of bartering or payment for such information flies in the face of the spirit of cyberspace, which is that it is a frontier that is meant to be explored, not a service controlled by corporations.[6]

■ Zero Tolerance for Interruptions. The high crime of interrupting a hacker during his craft should be punishable by a lobotomy. In the corporate world, it becomes harder and harder for hackers to keep their focus when other people are running around asking questions, pulling them into meetings, or simply shooting the breeze.

---

[6] Hackers who have taken the law into their own hands and broken into secured networks are referred to in the technical community as *crackers*. Their antics have led to countless acts of lost information, disruptions, and just plain bad manners!

The Hacker Cuisine

Food is often the only interruption that is tolerated in the hacker world. It is a welcomed break that permits the hacker to recharge. In most cases, the hacker will continue to work or at least continue to think about bugs and programming while he eats. Other times, he will banter with his fellow hackers about life out in cyberspace, recent episodes on T.V. or the wisdom of a particular technology.

Where the hacker's working world is filled with precision and great attention to detail, the hacker's food is not. It is meant to be fun. And the food the hacker craves is *hacker cuisine*.

The Nosebag

Hackers enjoy a wide assortment of ethnic foods and styles, but it is hacker cuisine, also known as *cyberchow*, *technogrub*, or to the old-timers simply *the nosebag*, that they eat while in cyberspace or in their brief respites between hacking. Hacker food uses recognizable conventions and ingredients, but its hallmarks are its large portions, quick preparation times, and unpredictable outcomes. An example of hacker cuisine is Twinkie Casserole, a fun dessert often served at hacker get-togethers.

Twinkie Casserole

 There is nothing like a large casserole for dessert, especially after a main course that did not quite go over with your crowd. Keep the ingredients for this dessert on hand for such an emergency. Presentation is everything with this dish. Each scrumptious layer will be a surprise for your guests.

2 dozen	Twinkies
1 large jar	caramel topping
1 bag	miniature marshmallows
1 large jar	hot fudge sauce
1 tsp.	cinnamon
dash	brown sugar
1 large bag	Oreos

1. Line the bottom of a casserole dish or a large plate with the Twinkies.
2. Pour the caramel topping evenly over the Twinkies and smooth with a knife.
3. Pour the miniature marshmallows over the top of the caramel until it is completely hidden.
4. Pour the hot fudge over the marshmallows.
5. Sprinkle the spices over the hot fudge.
6. Layer the Oreos on top of the casserole.
7. Serve immediately.

SERVES: 2 or 3

Hackers can become completely unglued over meals. They can consume large quantities in short amounts of time or snack on survival quantities of chips and fries as they rummage around hyperspace at night.

Hacker cuisine has a no-holds-barred approach. Maybe it seems crazy to non-hackers, but to hackers it is one more way life has been changed by technology. Hackers are no longer satisfied with the products of the past, the older technologies of food preparation, or the standard bland food combinations. Old-style recipes take too long and do not produce anything that hackers haven't seen or eaten before. So what's the point of doing all that work?

Hackers are simply not going to spend huge chunks of time over a stove making meals, but this does not mean they cannot prepare great food. A little basic training in opening cans and simple, spoon-in-the-bowl mixing is all the technique they need. After all, the food industry has evolved from legions of grandmothers cooking up chili to assembly lines that crank out sagans[7] of burgers, Twinkies, jams, and jellies each year. Each of these products is made and packaged immaculately. Have you ever seen a defective Twinkie or a can of Spam that did not taste the same?

They've gotten cooking and food preparation down to a science. Why reinvent the wheel? It is silly to think that amateurs should be concocting

---

[7] Billions and billions.

consommés, béchamel sauces, and elaborate suspensions that are available at our corner stores in a fraction of the time—and at a fraction of the cost. Some people may argue that it is somehow better to do the work yourself, but they are deluded. Conventional food preparation is costly, a waste of time, and frustrating. The final product turns out about one time in five.

Hackers are not interested in waiting for their dinners. They want their grub, and they want it now! Hackers believe that boiling, frying, broiling, roasting, steaming, and so on are outdated. Hacker cuisine takes on a new form of food preparation: combining.

Wherever and whenever it happens, hacker cuisine is intense snacking: Dinner is a snack of extended duration, between-meal snacks are usually referred to as lunch, and a hacker's favorite after-dinner activity is sleeping. The cuisine itself is difficult to define. Hackers like it, which should be fair warning. It is a type of creative combining—at once sloppy, large, and fun—like Shamu on Ex-Lax.

The Rules

Here are the basic rules of hacker cuisine.

■ There Are No Rules. Hacker cooks blend different ingredients with no thought to the end product or intestinal consequences. Spontaneity is the norm; mistakes are frequent, but hardly anyone notices. The details of the meal do not matter. If there is too much salt or not enough whiz, no one is going to send the food back to the kitchen. If you are concerned about details such as whether the meal is going to turn out, then you may be frustrated by hacker cuisine. As with good jazz, improvisation is essential.

■ Quick Before We Faint! Hackers have been in hyperspace most of the day. For them, waiting an extra five minutes when you are coming down from a caffeine high is sheer torture. They lose interest as well as consciousness if the dish is not on the table ready to go before their legs buckle.

■ Cymbal Crash! Hacker food fills your taste buds. Like popcorn and nachos at a movie, hacker food is the perfect complement to a night-long session of hacking. It must have texture and spice and maintain base sensory stimulation for long periods of time. It must have the same effect as a cymbal crash at a bris—sudden, unexpected, with everyone checking their pants for parts.

■ Give Us Mountains. We are not talking about small portions here. If you have to scrape around for the food at the bottom of the dish, it is not enough. Eating from large bowls or pans is commonplace for hackers, and usually it is done in front of the tube. Give a hacker mountains and mountains of food. If he cannot finish it, he'll save it for another meal or eat it anyway.

Hackers do not eat to satisfy the minimum daily nutritional requirements on the sides of boxes. They're here to pig out on a grand scale; to have le Grand Buffet; to eat until it kills them. Eating, like hacking, must be done with complete abandon. Preparing food, like hacking, must be done quickly, efficiently, and with re-usable ingredients.

Elements of hacker style can be summarized by three basic principles:

- ■ Eat until you drop.
- ■ Eat what you drop.
- ■ Enjoy first—ask questions later.

Batterie de Cuisine

Most hackers find that preparing food is instinctive—that they are born knowing how to mix food together in pleasing combinations. In many ways, playing in mud was their first exposure to doing this. There is really nothing to preparing hacker cuisine. However, to do so, you will need some tools of the trade, your batterie de cuisine, so to speak.

The Spoon

The most important cooking tool in the hacker arsenal is the spoon, and so you should give some thought to choosing the best type of spoon. Wooden, metal, and plastic spoons are available in many kitchen stores. Choose a wooden spoon if you have

pans that are Teflon and you want to avoid eating the carcinogenic flakes scraped up by a metal spoon. Spoon sizes range from a puny two inches in length to clearly unwieldy yard-long ladles.

In determining the optimal spoon size, remember that you will be using it to remove ingredients from cans. So, you must first find the width that is most desirable. Consider the diameter of the cans that you plan to use. Also, do not purchase any spoon that you cannot comfortably fit in your mouth. After all, you may find yourself eating with the same spoon with which you cooked. A spoon around three inches in width is the most practical.

The length and balance of the spoon are also important. If it is too short, you may not be able to reach either the pots on the stove or your mouth when you are hacking. The spoon should be approximately one foot long with good balance. If the balance is not correct, you may end up dropping Spam Soup (page 62) on the keyboard more often than is necessary. When selecting your primary spoon, feel its weight in your hands. Make sure it has the balance that you prefer—weighted more toward the handle to counterbalance large portions on the spoon side. Try eating with the spoon if the store permits. Remember: The right spoon can save you from a lot of embarrassing situations.

Finally, though you should not have to pay more than five dollars for a good spoon, shop around. Don't buy the first spoon you see. After all, this is not an impulse buy!

Emergency Utensils

There are times when eating simply interferes with hacking, yet in a state of frenzy you may need to resort to eating with anything that is at hand. The only way to handle these emergency situations is to grab whatever implements are nearby. Some suggestions:

■ *Slide rule.* Yes, these memorabilia of yesteryear can once again serve a useful purpose. For those hard-to-reach dishes, extend the rule's middle tongue to the desired length; then, with the hairline placed at the farthest point for extra scooping area, dip into your favorite meal. Retract the middle tongue to avoid lodging components of your slide rule in your esophagus.

■ *Flowchart templates.* These arcane design tools can be used both as dippers and to scrape remnants of meals from bowls. The best templates are the larger models. When scooping, make sure that you do not lose too much food through the cutouts.

■ *Corrupted floppies.* Instead of discarding floppy disks that fail to be formatted, tape a few spares to the side of your monitor for those unpredictable emergencies. By grasping the metal protector, you can use these floppies to scoop and spread meals.

The Can Opener

The next item that is absolutely necessary is an electric can opener. If you are serious about preparing hacker cuisine, invest in a large, industrial-size can opener, one that is able to open large cans. The magnets on top that hold the cans in place are usually much stronger, akin to the kind used at junkyards to move cars. In addition, the gears that turn the cans should be able to grasp and hold a quarter. This is always a good test for strength. Finally, the circular blades must be able to pierce the seals on survival-size cans of food.

When shopping for a can opener, it is always valuable to bring along a large can of your favorite food. In fact, going to your appliance shop at lunchtime can kill two birds with one stone: First, you can test-drive one of the can openers on display, and second, you can have lunch while negotiating the price with the store clerk.[8] Set your opened can on the counter, pull up a chair, and have a frank discussion about price, terms of the warranty, and so forth.

The Microwave

The key to any hacker dish is getting it from can to tabletop in the least amount of time. The microwave is the perfect appliance for this. Old-fashioned

---

[8] I have used this technique often. I have found that pork and beans in the gallon survival size offers the best test for can openers.

methods of cooking with pots or ovens pale in comparison to this space-age marvel.

In determining which microwave will best suit your style of cooking, keep in mind that most dishes call for setting the microwave on its top setting (high) and blasting the food until it steams. Although having additional · settings on the microwave may come in handy, it is the actual wattage of the appliance that is paramount. The higher the wattage, the more desirable the unit. Use a recent edition of *Consumer Reports* to prepare a short list of microwave manufacturers. Sort this list by the maximum outputs the microwaves can produce. Limit your list to your three choices within your price range.

With list in hand, the most efficient way to choose a microwave is the Popcorn Test, as follows:

1. Take a large jar of unpopped popcorn and a number of large storage baggies with you as you make your rounds to local appliance stores.
2. For each microwave you want to test, ladle a cup of raw popcorn into a baggie and place it into the microwave.
3. Set each timer to ten minutes on high and start the microwaves in unison.
4. Time how long it takes for all of the kernels to pop. Microwaves vary in their maximum power and the efficiency of their design. Buy the microwave with the shortest pop time.
5. Eat the popcorn.

The full test should not take longer than a lunch break, and in most cases, there will be enough popcorn left over for dinner. Remember to shut off the microwaves when the popcorn has completely popped. If you don't, you run the risk of blowing the microwave doors off their hinges. The kernels may also shrivel.

The Bowl

The bowl is one of the most versatile items in your hacker arsenal. As with any good computer code, it is reusable. Not only can it be used to prepare the recipes, but with very little thought, the same bowl can be used to serve the finished product. Most hacker recipes are truly one-bowl dishes.

The bowl has evolved to the dish of choice for its ability to accommodate most types of hacker cuisine, from dips such as Roughage Whip (page 40) to more formal dinner entrees such as Mashed Spaghetti (page 48) and Macaroni and Beef Jerky Casserole (page 59). The bowl is ideal for one-handed eating when you are in hack mode and can be balanced on a lap or stomach for casual dining in front of the tube.

In selecting the right bowl for your kitchen, keep in mind that the bowl must be large enough to handle most of your meals, and, of course, it must be microwave-safe. So, most salad and soup bowls will simply not cut the mustard. Look instead to mixing bowls, which come in a variety of sizes and materials. Most are made to handle large amounts. It is suggested that you buy larger bowls, which give you room for expansion as your appetite increases. You must be able to mix ingredients around easily without losing too much over the rim.

It is recommended that you take a survival can of pork and beans to your local kitchen shop and test-drive the bowls. Simply ladle the entire can contents into the bowls of choice and swish them around. Make sure that the ingredients all move in the same direction and remain in the bowl even when your stirring is most frantic. (After all, you will prepare many meals while in a desperate, frenzied state, so it is best to emulate real-life conditions as best you can.) Also, test how easily the full bowl can be moved. Take a short run with a full bowl to another department, such as men's suits.[9] Keep the contents as level as you can, then make an abrupt about-face and return to the kitchen department.

If you managed to keep all of the ingredients in the bowl, then it will most likely suit your purposes. If you ended up marking too many of the suits when you turned around, you may want to try a larger bowl. Check the carpeting along the route you took to see if the bowl leaked too heavily. In these lean economic times, store managers are usually quite accommodating, so continue your tests until you are forcibly removed from the store.

---

[9] If you have never been to this department in the store, ask directions or choose a more familiar department. Make sure the department is located a fair distance so you can test the bowl's portability.

Now, with spoon and bowl in hand, you are ready to begin preparing classic hacker dishes.

Entertaining

Until recently, hacker cuisine has always been served to hackers. For these veterans, not much in the way of an explanation or planning has been required. The mere presence of the food has been enough to inspire long sessions of dipping and enjoyment. However, as more digital neophytes are being exposed to the delights of the Net, late-night hacker chats, and other forms of hacker culture, so too has appeared a growing curiosity of outsiders to eat like a hacker.

Jumping into the hacker bowl, so to speak, is not as easy as it sounds.

For hackers, there is a new concept: entertaining. Whether it is for a homogeneous group of fellow hackers fresh from hack mode or for a special guest, entertaining requires a little more thought and planning than a normal hacker meal.

For That Special Evening

Contrary to popular belief, hackers are interested in developing a special relationship. Dating is a foreign concept to many die-hard hackers, but still, chowing down with that special someone can make for a fun evening, and hacker meals are an excellent way to break the ice.

Although lining up a special guest and inviting him or her to dinner can be frustrating, once your guest has accepted, you are home free. You will need to decide where your guest will sit and how cluttered or uncluttered you want your apartment to be on the first meeting. The rule of thumb is to keep the living room, bathroom, and bedroom recognizable. It may set the evening back if your guest mistakes the living room for the bathroom, although not a great deal of harm is done if the bedroom is mistaken for the living room. Nevertheless, cleanliness is tantamount to a solid relationship.

If you are incorrigibly sloppy, you are on very shaky ground. In these situations, only large quantities of booze will help bridge your guest's instinctive revulsion. You may suggest meeting your guest at your corner bar first, perhaps because your place is a "little hard to find" (not to mention stomach). This suggestion may be greeted as wonderfully considerate. Upon entering your digs, keep the lights low and move your guest quickly to the table. Do not linger in your living room if it is hard to find the couch.

Preparing for Dinner

Apart from general appearance, you will need to spend some time on the table setting and menu. Do not go hog wild on the table setting. Your efforts won't make much difference anyway. Make sure that there are two plates, two knives, two forks, and two spoons. Also, use real napkins and not paper towels.

No matter what you are planning to eat, the fact that you supply utensils is soothing and reminds your nonhacker guest that, although everything

Obnoxious Company

If a guest refuses to take hints and continues relating stories of the Jackson Five or the advantages of paper tape, you may find yourself as host in the uncomfortable position of getting rid of him or her.

There is no easy way. Dropping more hints usually will fuel the fire. The easiest way to dislodge a guest—especially when you have more important hacking to do—is the following:

- Wait for the first sentence that sounds like a punch line or a mildly controversial statement.
- Immediately get to your feet and say, "That's it! You're out of here."
- Grab the guest by the shirt and drag him or her to the door. Do not bother to explain.
- Lock your front door; ignore all knocks or any subsequent phone calls. Put those headphones on and zone out.

else in the evening may be a little difficult to swallow, at least you are another member of the civilized world. This will be heartening.

After you've got the table set, it's time to decide on your menu. This is probably the most important decision you will make. You will need to decide on drinks, a main course, and a dessert, at minimum. The combination is important, because flavors of one course can complement or detract from those of another. Here are some suggestions:

■ *Think up a theme for the evening*. It may be as innocuous as "Italian food" or as intriguing as "Einstein's autopsy," but let your imagination rule. Stay clear of themes such as "show and tell" or "doctor," because the menu choices will tend to be too anatomical, and your guest may take offense.

■ *Choose a menu based on a recent current event*. Remember how much fun election-day potlucks were? Spend an hour or so in front of the television. Any fast-breaking news event may trigger a great theme. Stay away from themes concerning accidents, assassination attempts, or particularly gruesome war footage, which may put a damper on the evening. Choose something like "save our rain forests" or "cut the budget." Themes such as "soup kitchen" have been popular with hackers over the years, as have "Klingon picnic," "vegetarian circuit design," "finger-painting," and "the art of Willem de Kooning."

■ *Use free association to pick the menu*. This method has been used in mental hospitals with great results, although usually it is not applied to menus. Still, it can produce some very unique combinations and should be given a chance if all else fails.

Once you have your menu prepared, whip it together.

Adjusting Recipes for Your Guests

In general, do not adjust your recipes. In the first place, you will never know exactly what your guest will like. If they have never had hacker cuisine before, minor tweaking won't make much difference anyway.

If they've had hacker cuisine before, you can always keep an extra jar of Cheese Whiz handy or leave the ice cream carton on the table. This way, they can help themselves to more.

The rule of thumb is to make your dinner as if you were the only one eating it. In fact, no matter how hard you try to make dinner to the liking of your guest, you may still end up being the only one eating it, so you might as well enjoy yourself. Life is too short for mind reading.

Preparing the Meal

Preparing the meal should not take long. Here are some rules of thumb:

- If you have botched a recipe, just change the name.
- If you have forgotten an ingredient, just leave it out unless it was the main ingredient (then use the above rule).
- If you've produced an ill-tasting or foul-smelling mess, serve it as a dip before dinner. If its odor is too strong, explain that it is from Zimbabwe or Luxembourg, where tangy food is preferred.

Remember that half the fun of the evening starts with preparing the food. If you are having a good time, it will show in the final dish.

Serving Tips

In recent times, serving has been a way of heightening a meal's appeal. There are wonderful serving bowls in bright colors, and at finer restaurants dishes are brought to the table under silver covers. This treatment adds to the suspense, while keeping the food warm.

With hacker cuisine, serving technique doubles as a distraction. You do not want your guests to scrutinize the meal too closely. The food has suffered enough in the kitchen: It has been tortured, squeezed, slapped, and zapped until its integrity has been utterly defeated. Combine this with the fact that the food in general is rather ugly, and you will see why many hackers consider serving a covert action.

Of course, if you are eating by yourself, you can eat straight from the mixing bowl. With guests you must remember to keep the meal warm. While there is nothing like eating cold bean dip, your guests may like to have it warm occasionally, and ensuring that the dish stays that way from microwave to computer (or table) is an important courtesy of serving. Using a lid or setting a plate on top of the mixture during transport is a good practice.

Prior to taking the dish out to the table, look at it. This inspection will be your last opportunity to remove any offending objects (including organic matter, loose pharmaceuticals, or old telephone messages). Carefully lift any undesirable items from the dish and set aside.

You may want to add some garnish at this point. Doing this is highly risky, however, since it will suggest to your guests that the dish did not turn out quite right. They will be asking themselves, "Why is this garnish here?" Garnish is the first indication that something is amiss. However, if you feel you must dress up the dish, there are some basic rules of thumb:

- When in doubt, use parsley. If you do not have parsley, use the darkest lettuce you have. Chop it into parsley-sized pieces, then spread sparingly on top.
- For most dishes, use a dollop of the original ingredients on top. For example, scatter some popcorn on top of your Popcorn Frittata (page 55), or some

cheese on your Fish Stick Stir-Fry (page 49). This activity may require venturing back to the garbage and scraping leftovers from the cans, but it is well worth the time.

■ Where all else fails, use Oreos as garnish. They tend to go with any dish, and everyone likes them.

With your garnish in place, it is best to move the dish quickly to its final destination. Here are some basic serving guidelines:

■ Wherever possible, use the original bowl or pot. This is especially important for pots. Although they may be rather messy to bring to a table (or desk), they retain heat, so your food will stay warmer longer. When necessary, protect your table with an old magazine to prevent burn marks.

■ Wipe off your bowls or pots to keep your hands and the hands of your guests cleaner.

■ Bring your primary spoon to the table and use it as the serving spoon. (Wipe it clean first, if necessary.)

■ Place the meal as close to your guests as possible for purposes of good etiquette.

■ For an especially ugly meal, strike up a conversation as you are carrying in the meal. The more controversial the conversation, the better it distracts your guests. As alternatives, ask your guests to change channels or CDs to steer them away from the table as you set the meal down. In short, the more diversions, the better.

Once the meal is on the table, you can relax. The worst part of serving is over. You may either offer to serve your guests (which is rather time-consuming but polite) or simply let people know that they can dig in any time. A simple "well, let's eat" will suffice. Coaxing guests to try a dish or two may be a little tricky for first-timers, but be patient. Once they have actually tasted the food, you will find that their inhibitions will completely disappear.

The keys to hacker cooking are simplicity and creativity—the mainstays of any cook's arsenal. Some words of advice in this regard:

■ Don't do anything you don't have to do.

■ If you don't have what you need, substitute. It'll turn out better anyway.

Dips

Basic Techniques

IN MUCH THE same way that sauces are the culinary foundation of French cooking, dips are the elemental building blocks of hacker cuisine. After all, the more complicated dishes, such as Potato Chip Lasagna (see page 47), are simply the dips and chips mixed together. Where better to describe the basic techniques of hacker cuisine? Once you have mastered the subtle arts of spooning, stirring, and zapping, the rest is easy.

Spooning

Transferring mountains of food from one container to another is a basic skill that most hackers overlook. The objective is to accomplish the transfer with the minimum amount of spillage and in the shortest amount of time. The spoon is used to control the width of the spill over the lip. Especially when you are transferring portions from a larger bowl into a smaller one, your accuracy will be very important.

Starting with your two containers as close together as possible, grasp the first (or source) container, tilt it over the second (or destination) container, and pour, using the spoon as a means of controlling the flow. If you are a beginner, your ratio of spilled to spooned food may be high. However, as you become more facile, your spilled-to-spooned ratio should decrease, until finally you are able to transfer the entire mixture where you want it.

The classic way to control the spill is to rotate the source bowl slightly while using the spoon to push the mixture over the rim. As you rotate, the trailing edge of the spill will be continually forced in the direction of the rotation, while the leading edge will spread less due to friction. In the meantime, the spoon is moving the food as fast as it can into the new bowl.

If you are spooning out of a can or a smaller bowl, the technique can be abbreviated. Instead of pouring the mixture, you can usually turn the can

21

completely over, give it a solid thwack, and the entire contents will land in the destination bowl. (This is referred to as *jamming.*) If the can holds solid food—like refried beans or Spam—this technique works very well.

Finally, if the can is too big and you are having a hard time getting a grip, dig the spoon into the food and, with a circular motion, remove as much with your spoon as you can. Then, with the snap of your wrist, slop the contents of the spoon into the bowl (for obvious reasons, this is referred to as *slopping*). Try to move the food with a minimum of scoops.

In any spooning variant, speed is the key. The faster you can get the food where you want it, the sooner you will eat.

Stirring

After you have transferred the basic ingredients into a large bowl, it is time to stir. First check to see that everything is in the bowl. Especially if you are feeding others, check your recipe and compare it to what you see in the bowl. Remove anything that moves.

There are two basic procedures for stirring: with and without your spoon. Stirring with your hands is often more efficient and more controllable than stirring with a spoon, especially when the final mixture requires a mushy consistency.

To decide whether to use a spoon, look at the recipe's ingredients. If you are going to break these ingredients apart, then using your hands is more practical: You will be able to feel the different textures in the mixture and know when to separate them. Also, determine whether you want a loose mix with larger intact lumps. Using your hands will facilitate a rougher mix. For example, in Loose Pudding Surprise (page 74), you will want puddles of chocolate milk to be suspended in the pudding.

The techniques of hand stirring are:

■ *Squeezing.* Grab the food in either hand and squeeze. The ingredients should squirt out through your fingers with a flatulent sound. Rapid squeezing should sound like a train in mud. Squeezing is a great way of mixing your food: It not only produces satisfying sounds to work by but also builds up your forearm muscles.

■ *Slapping.* Take a chunk of food on a flattened palm and slap it into the remaining mixture. This technique is also referred to as "torturing your food." (See below, *slamming.*)

■ *Slamming* (emphatic variation of *slapping*). Grab a large portion of the ingredients in both hands and slam them down again, roughly in the same spot. Slamming's major drawback is that it does not achieve good mixing. It is mostly useful for getting your frustrations out at the end of a bad day.

■ *Finger stirring.* This is obviously microstirring. When you find little pockets of ingredients, for example, some Cheez Whiz that refuses to blend into the rest of the batch, whip that portion with a single finger, using a circular motion.

- *Peeking.* Remove your hands from the concoction and visually inspect it for any active life forms. Pull it apart, pushing aside any large pieces, and examine the minutiae. Get your nose as close to the mixture as possible so that you can detect any unwelcome smells.
- *Shiatsu.* This classic Asian massage technique works wonders on hard-to-stir portions. Using your fingers, push and pull at the mixture as if it were a couple of lumpy shoulders. An occasional slap or punch is also good.

Forearm squeegee

In mixing a dip, your counter may end up with more of the basic ingredients than your bowl. The simple solution is to put on your glasses. However, hackers have come up with a clever solution:

1. Roll your sleeve up to above the elbow.
2. With one sweeping movement, place your forearm on the counter and squeegee everything on the counter into the bowl.
3. Wipe your forearm on anything handy.

Presto! Your mixture is once again in the bowl, and you are ready to move ahead.

If you want to pulverize, chop, smash, or indiscriminately mix, then the spoon is your ideal instrument. Keep your primary spoon handy for these jobs. Follow these steps:

- *Basic stirring.* Grasp the bowl firmly by the rim. If your hands are slimy, use rubber gloves or place your forearm across the top of the bowl. Keep the bowl steady. With your spoon, smash the large chunks of food against the bottom. Then, with a scooping action, scrape them off again. Continue doing this until the larger chunks disintegrate.
- *Whipping.* With fierce, circular strokes, stir the ingredients together rapidly and without mercy. If you are in the northern hemisphere, stir counterclockwise to take full advantage of the Coriolis effect. (In the southern hemisphere, stir clockwise.) Whip the mixture as quickly as you can. Keep in mind that stirring can be an aerobic exercise.[1]
- *Chopping.* Use chopping when you discover unwanted lumps. With the edge of the spoon, chop the mixture with short vertical motions. Alternatively, you can smash these chunks against the side of the bowl. Check to see if any mixture is stuck on the bottom of the bowl. If so, scrape it off with the spoon. Squeegee any of the mixture off your countertops.

---

[1]If you are interested in adding a cardiovascular exercise to your food preparation, jog in place as you stir.

■ *Thwacking*. Use the bottom of your spoon to hit the mixture hard. You will hear a loud thwack.

The final product should not betray any of the original ingredients. With proper stirring, the mixtures will have muddled colors, hard-to-describe textures, and unusual odors. If you find that the end product looks slightly disgusting, then you are probably doing everything correctly.

Zapping

Warming is an art form. Too often restaurants—especially fast food restaurants—overlook the importance of microwaving food for the right amount of time. They will prepare most of the dishes properly and then proceed to zap the rolls for fifteen minutes on high. The rolls will feel soft to the touch but inside be blazing hot and inedible. The roll adheres to the first tongue it touches.

Hackers refer to warming food with a microwave as *zapping*. There is no better way to learn about zapping than by trial and error. Experiment with the microwave so that you get a feel for how much damage zapping can cause. For example, take a flour tortilla and place it into a microwave. Zap it for ten seconds, then take it out and examine the temperature and texture. Is the tortilla hot enough? If not, pop it back in for another ten seconds, and continue doing this until you get the right results.

Experiment with bean dip, Cheez Whiz, frozen hamburgers, and so on. Keep zapping until you begin to pick up a sense of how long you need to use the microwave for different ingredients. Here are some guidelines:

■ Always use the high setting. It makes no sense to try to defrost or warm in a microwave. Microwaves were designed for quick cooking, so blast your food.

■ Use the times indicated on most recipes as a rough approximation of the zap time. Set the zap time as indicated in the recipes, but then listen for popping sounds or explosions coming from your microwave. These sounds usually

Squirting your dips

It is usually not recommended that you play with your food unless it is part of mixing the meal. However, sometimes the easiest way to get food to your mouth is by filling both hands with dips, grasping your hands together, and squirting the mixture into your mouth. Use the same technique as you do in a swimming pool.

Aim is important: There are a lot of bad accidents that have been sold as modern art.

indicate that the dish is done. Remove quickly and hose down the inside of the microwave.

- If you think of it, stop the zapping midway through and stir the dish. This pausing technique is usually very helpful for casseroles, soups, or dishes with a high liquid content. You will find that the edges heat up pretty quickly, leaving the middle of the dish ice cold. Although some hackers like this temperature differential, a quick stir results in a more consistently warm dish.

  The problem with stirring during the cooking time is that you hate to wait by the microwave. Some hackers set their microwaves to half the zap time so they get a reminder to stir the food when the microwave beeps. However, more often than not, this also is too complicated. In the end, you will probably not do any of this stirring, so it is best not to get your hopes up.

- To test the food's temperature, stick your finger into the middle of it. If the food is underzapped, its center will be cold. If the food is overzapped, you will see blisters. Adjust your cooking time accordingly.

- When removing the dish from the microwave, always use pot holders. If you do not have any, then it is best to perfect a "juggling" technique for moving the dish to the table. Lightly toss the dish up in the air (this will momentarily cool your fingers) and alternate hands.

- Never use metal containers in a microwave— not even as a joke.

Cattle Dip

Cattle dip has long been a Texan favorite, combining the great taste of beans and beef jerky into an easy-to-chew dip. This dip is great to serve at barbecues, but inappropriate for the geriatric population because the beef jerky does not really soften that much.

1 large can	bean dip
1 can	pinto beans
3 sticks	beef jerky, chopped
1 jar	Cheez Whiz
1 packet	onion soup
2 large	chilies, chopped
1 can	chopped olives
1 can	corn
1 can	Spam, diced
1 tsp.	soy sauce

Soy Sauce

Soy Sauce is one of the staples of a hacker diet. Brewed from pressings of soybeans, this mixture is rich in essential amino acids (only methionine is lacking, and this can be supplied from pretzels or corn chips). It provides the essential salty taste to most dishes and should be purchased in bulk.

1. Combine the ingredients in a large bowl and stir until lumpy. Let the mixture stand for 10 minutes (if you are not too hungry).
2. Serve immediately or chill overnight.

SERVES: 2 OR 3

Hacker Fondue with Pork Rinds

For cheese lovers, the classic Swiss fondue has been updated for quick preparation and a more modern taste.

2 pounds	Cheddar cheese
1 package	Velveeta cheese
1/2 cup	sour cream
dash	pepper
dash	salt
1 bag	pork rinds

1. Chop the Cheddar cheese in 1/2″ strips and place into a large bowl. Cut in the Velveeta cheese and mash.
2. Microwave cheese mixture for 5–6 minutes until melted.
3. Stir thoroughly into a smooth consistency. Add remaining ingredients and serve very hot with the pork rinds.

SERVES: 2 OR 3

Variations:

Hacker Fondue with Cheese Strips. Serve with cheese strips alongside.

26

Hacker Fondue with Slim Jims. Instead of serving with cheese strips, use spicy Slim Jims for a great surprise.

Five-Minute Quiche Dip

This quick dish is a variation on standard quiche without the hours of mixing and baking. Milk, eggs, and cheese are replaced with unflavored gelatin and Cheez Whiz to approximate the same taste and consistency. Serve as a main course or as a dip with chips.

2 packets	unflavored gelatin
1 cup	chicken stock
1 bottle	Cheez Whiz
1 bottle	mushrooms
1 can	corn
1 can	Spam, diced
1 can	chopped olives
2 tsp.	soy sauce
dash	pepper
dash	salt
1 frozen	pie crust, premade

1. Combine the gelatin and chicken stock. Zap in the microwave for 3 minutes.
2. In a bowl, combine all remaining ingredients except the pie crust.
3. Pour mixture into pie crust.
4. Let quiche cool until runny. Serve warm (for firmer quiche, store in the refrigerator overnight).

SERVES: 2 OR 3

Variation:

Bean Quiche. Stir a can of refried beans in with the other ingredients.

Bean Barrel

 This classic recipe combines unique flavors of the Southwest with massive amounts of beans for a high-fiber, satisfying dip.

1 large can	**bean dip**
1 can	**pinto beans**
1 can	**refried beans**
1 can	**pork and beans**
1/2 jar	**salsa**
2 large	**chilies, chopped**
1 can	**chopped olives**
1 can	**corn**
1 small can	**tomato sauce**
1 dollop	**sour cream (for garnish)**
1 tsp.	**soy sauce**
dash	**chili pepper (to taste)**

1. Combine the first four ingredients in a large bowl and mash until the consistency of loose refried beans.
2. Add remaining ingredients and stir.
3. Serve immediately with tortillas or chips, or chill overnight.

SERVES: 2 TO 4

Bean dip and your carpeting

Bean dips make nasty stains in carpeting, especially after they have dried and been ground into the nap for several months. Although removing any spilled food from your floors when they first occur is the best solution, this almost never happens. We tend to be much too hungry to stop what we are doing.

Here are some suggestions to follow if neglected dip begins to make bald spots (which can become potentially slippery in inclement weather) in your carpet:

■ Use a little warm water and a Brillo pad to remove any excess caking. Dip the Brillo pad into the water, shake out the excess and scrub the offending blotch. Make sure that you do not scrub off the actual carpeting, or you will be left with a permanent bald spot.

■ When the spill occurs, get out a spray bottle of cleaner (such as 409). Spray the spot right away. Remind any guests of these spots, or you will find more people than usual sitting on their hands.

If all else fails, turn these matted areas of your carpet into putting greens. A golf flag at each site and borrowed miniature golf clubs can provide hours of fun.

Mouth-Wrenching Salsa

This dip is not for the meek. It is the hottest salsa that can be legally served without written warnings on the side of the bowl. For guests unaccustomed to this type of food, make sure that you have plenty of beer handy (yogurt is also a good fire quencher).

1 large can	**salsa**
1 large	**onion, chopped**
3 raw	**garlic cloves, coarsely chopped**
5	**jalapeño chilies, chopped**
1 can	**green chilies, chopped**
3 raw	**paloma chilies, chopped**
1 can	**chopped olives**
1/2 can	**corn**
1 small can	**tomato sauce**
1 dollop	**sour cream (for garnish)**
1 tsp.	**soy sauce**
1 tsp.	**chili pepper, (to taste)**
1 tsp.	**black pepper**
dash	**salt**

1. Combine the ingredients in a large bowl and stir until the mixture is lumpy and thick. For extra thickness, add bread crumbs.
2. Serve immediately with tortillas or chips, or chill overnight.

      SERVES: **2 TO 4**

Canned Veggie Curry Dip

For a light summer dip, combine cans of mixed vegetables in a sour cream base for a refreshing taste.

This dip is a variation on a Buddhist dip that usually

Hacker Dreams

Very little is known about hacker dreams, since they have largely gone uncharted by the likes of Freud, Jung, and Ron Jeremy. However, it is common knowledge that most top-notch hackers debug in their sleep; that is, they continue to program while sleeping.

The author has had a number of vivid dreams in which troubled modules have been run, error messages generated, and actual lines of code traced—all in the dream. Upon waking, the author rushed to the computer and found the exact lines that appeared in his dream. Sure, enough: These lines were the cause of the problems.

This method of debugging is infallible, although it can be hard to control, since the unconscious mind can place large tubs of dip or mountains of chips alongside the screens at night. Still, it is a wonderful exercise.

uses curries and freshly grown vegetables. Serve with crackers or celery sticks.

1 container	sour cream
1 packet	vegetable dip mix
1 can	peas
1 can	okra
1 can	chopped olives
1 can	corn
1 can	Spam, diced (optional)
2 tbsp.	curry powder
1 tsp.	soy sauce
dash	pepper
dash	salt

1. Combine the ingredients in a large bowl and stir gently. Rough stirring can break the peas and okra. Make sure the curry powder is combined well, since it has a tendency to form lumps that can cause breathing problems if eaten.
2. Serve immediately, or chill overnight.

SERVES: 2 OR 3

Handcream

This sweet dip has long been a favorite at parties. Set out with all of the standard dips, it combines vanilla pudding and a touch of mayonnaise for a creamy candy surprise. This dip goes best with salty chips or crackers.

Wiping those fingers

There is nothing worse than a slippery keyboard, yet one of the unfortunate aspects of chips is their excess grease. Not that it does not taste great—it does—but a hacker's fingers can become perpetually coated with this unstoppable slime, and so too the keyboard. The handiest way to wipe your fingers is on your shirt, of course. (A simple lick or two, then a couple of swipes of your palms across your stomach, should rid you of the pesky lubricant.) However, there are a number of other options:

■ *Coke dunk.* Dip your fingertips into an icy glass of Coke or your favorite beverage. (Hot coffee is not recommended.)

■ *Discarded printouts.* If your recycling bin is close, grab the top sheet and use it as a hand towel. Return it to the bin. (This top sheet can withstand up to a dozen wipes, so it is the perfect solution for heavy dip days.)

■ *The Vitalis look.* If you have that wet look anyway, run your fingers through your hair. The grease actually can condition hair and minimize split ends. If your hair also tends to be greasy, this may not be a good solution, since you may be compounding the problem.

3 cups	vanilla pudding
1/2 cup	mayonnaise
1 pound	chocolate candy (such as M&M's or Reese's Pieces)
dash	black pepper for zest
dash	salt
dash	paprika (for garnish)

1. Combine all of the ingredients except the paprika in a large bowl and mix well. The pudding and mayonnaise should completely coat and cover the candy.
2. Shake the paprika on top.
3. Serve chilled.

SERVES: 2 TO 4

Mayonnaise Turkey Whip

Smoked turkey and mayonnaise have always been favorites of sandwich lovers. This unique dip blends these two tastes into a creamy dish that can be served with pumpernickel crackers or plain old corn chips.

2 packages	smoked deli turkey
3 cups	mayonnaise
1 tsp.	white or black pepper
dash	salt
dash	paprika (for garnish)

1. Place smoked turkey on a cutting board and chop into very fine pieces. Pour into a bowl.

2. Add the remaining ingredients and whip until smooth.
3. Serve chilled. Do not leave dip out too long, or it will spoil.

SERVES: 2 OR 3

Tuna Fish Dip

This is another wonderful mayonnaise dip that combines equal parts of tuna fish with mayonnaise. It is like eating a tuna fish sandwich without the bread.

2 cans	tuna fish
2 cups	mayonnaise
1 tsp.	white or black pepper
dash	salt
dash	paprika (for garnish)

1. Empty the tuna fish into a bowl and mash thoroughly with a fork until there are no large chunks.
2. Add the remaining ingredients and whip until smooth.
3. Serve chilled. Do not leave dip out too long, or it will spoil.

SERVES: 2 OR 3

Peanut Butter and Jelly Dip

Peanut butter dips have long been a mainstay of hacker get-togethers. The key with these classic dips is to make the peanut butter creamy enough to be

scooped onto chips or crackers. To do this, choose slightly runny peanut butter if you can find it (many health food stores stock a "raw" peanut butter in which the oil separates very easily from the rest of the peanut butter), but because this is not always readily available, this recipe includes some vegetable oil to loosen the mixture. The chilies and pepper add a great spiciness to the dip.

1 large jar	**peanut butter**
1/2 cup	**vegetable oil (for creamier dips)**
1 small can	**green chilies, chopped**
1 tsp.	**white or black pepper**
dash	**salt**
1 jar	**grape jelly**
handful	**nuts (for garnish)**

1. Combine all of the ingredients except the jelly and nuts in a large bowl. Whip until creamy.
2. Swirl in the jelly. Do not stir too much.
3. Scatter the nuts on top and serve chilled with crackers or chips.

SERVES: 2 OR 3

Sheep Dip

This sour cream-based dip originates in Australia, where it is served, like everything else, with large quantities of beer. Although rumored to have been used in a bind on sheep farms, this dip is very popular with almost any chip, pretzel, or cracker. It is normally served thick, in a large container or bucket.

1 container	**sour cream**
1 packet	**onion soup mix**
2 large	**chilies, chopped**
1 can	**chopped olives**
1 can	**corn**
1 can	**Spam, diced**
1 tbsp.	**chili powder (optional)**
1 tsp.	**soy sauce**
dash	**pepper**
dash	**salt**

1. Combine the ingredients in a large bowl and stir until lumpy and white. Add the chili powder for extra punch.
2. Serve immediately, or chill overnight.

SERVES: 2 OR 3

Peanut Butter Hot Fudge Dip

This classic dip marries the wonderful richness of chocolate and peanut butter. It may be served warm or chilled.

1 large jar	**peanut butter**
1/2 cup	**vegetable oil**
1/2 cup	**brown sugar**
1 pound	**chocolate candy**
1 cup	**chopped nuts (optional)**
dash	**salt**
1 jar	**hot fudge sauce**

1. Combine all of the ingredients except the hot fudge sauce in a large bowl. Whip until creamy.
2. Swirl in the hot fudge sauce. Do not stir too much.
3. Serve chilled, or zapped in the microwave, with chocolate bars or chips.

SERVES: 2 or 3

Lava Dip

 Sometimes after eating a heavy meat dish, you may hanker for something chocolate and sweet. This dip is just the thing. It has its roots in Swiss fondue, except that it has more chocolate and is usually eaten without fruit or ladled by itself into small serving dishes. Serve with crackers, chips, ice cream, or chocolate bars and plenty of napkins.

4 pounds	**chocolate candy**
2 jars	**hot fudge sauce**
1/2 tsp.	**brown sugar**
1 cup	**M&M's (for garnish)**
dash	**salt**

1. Combine all of the ingredients in a large bowl.
2. Zap in a microwave for 4 minutes or until all of the mixture has melted.
3. Stir until smooth.
4. Serve hot with chocolate bars or chips. Keep mixture warm for best results. Periodic zapping in the microwave will keep it loose and scoopable.

SERVES: 2 OR 3

Fried Rice Dip

 There is nothing as tasty as old fried rice that has lounged around in your refrigerator for days. Of course, you will want it to be roughly the same color as the original dish, but a quick zap in the microwave (with a little water) can bring it all back to life.

2 tbsp.	**water**
1 carton	**leftover fried rice**
1 cup	**sour cream**
1 packet	**onion soup mix**
1 can	**chopped olives**
2 tbsp.	**Cheez Whiz**
2 tbsp.	**vegetable oil**
2 tbsp.	**soy sauce**
dash	**pepper**
1/2 bag	**frozen peas, thawed**

1. Add the water to the fried rice and zap in a microwave until the rice is moist and regains its original consistency. (Do not use leftover white rice even you've collected enough to fill a stadium. White rice tends to dilute the dip's taste, so save it for the No-Op Dip [see page 35] if you need to use it up.)
2. Combine all of the remaining ingredients except the peas in a large bowl and mash gently with a fork. The rice should stick together.
3. Add the peas and stir until the mixture is colorful

and appealing. Be patient. This may take a while.

4. Serve warm with rice cakes or leftover tortillas.

SERVES: 2 OR 3

Leftover Mashed Potato Dip

Mashed potatoes can keep in the refrigerator for quite a while. With a little reconstructive therapy, old dry potatoes can be whipped into a moist batch as long as their color is approximately white. Just add milk and stir. However, for special occasions, you may want to add a little mayonnaise and sour cream to leftover mashed potatoes to make a real crowd pleaser. This combination tastes great, and you can serve leftovers as a side dish at your next meal. Try this dip with potato chips for the extreme potato treat.

4 cups	leftover mashed potatoes
1 cup	mayonnaise
1 cup	sour cream
2 tbsp.	vegetable oil
2 tbsp.	garlic salt
1 tbsp.	salt
2 tbsp.	water
dash	pepper
1 cup	crumbled potato chips (for texture)

1. Combine the ingredients in a large bowl and whip into a frenzy. Crumble in old potato chips

for added crunchiness. (Anything dry and crunchy will do; leftover sardines are also an intriguing substitute.)

2. Serve warm with chips or pretzels.

SERVES: 2 OR 3

Butter Dip

For that great butter taste, there is nothing better than the real thing. This dip is ideal to serve with bread sticks.

2 tbsp.	vegetable oil
1 tub	whipped butter or faux butter
dash	pepper

1. Stir the oil into the butter to soften it for dipping.

2. Zap in the microwave very briefly. If you zap this dish too long, you might need to serve it as a butter shake, so watch out.

3. Sprinkle with pepper and serve warm with chips or pretzels.

SERVES: 4 TO 6

Liverwurst and Anchovy Tub

This dip started out on pizza and finally found its way into a unique dip. Not everyone will appreciate the combination of liver and the saltiness of anchovies, but it is bound to make people step back. The secret

33

is to whip the liverwurst with a little mayonnaise to make it creamier, then to chop in the anchovies. Fish liver is a great source of vitamin A; liver and fish are doubly so.

3 tubes	**liverwurst**
2 tins	**anchovies, chopped**
dash	**pepper**
1/2 cup	**mayonnaise**

1. Whip the liverwurst, anchovies, pepper, and mayonnaise in a large bowl until soft.
2. Zap in the microwave very briefly.
3. Serve warm with chips or fish sticks.

SERVES: 4 TO 6

Paper Bag Surprise

Ever wonder what drunks carry around in those paper bags? I guess not. But anyway, this dish looks like old airplane glue and is sure to please even the most seen-it-all hacker.

1 cup	**mayonnaise**
1 cup	**sour cream**
1 can	**whole pinto beans**
1 packet	**vegetable dip mix**
2 tbsp.	**Cheez Whiz**
1 tbsp.	**chili pepper**
1 tsp.	**salt**
dash	**pepper**

1. Whip the ingredients in a large bowl until combined. Do not worry about breaking up the pinto beans. You're working for a battered character in this dip.
2. Zap in the microwave for a very short period of time.
3. Half-fill a bag with the mixture. Roll the sides of the bag down for easier access.
4. Serve warm with chips, or just use your fingers. If you have leftovers, you can easily set them out on a street corner and watch the derelicts enjoy.

SERVES: 4 TO 6

Fries and Ketchup Dip

There is nothing that beats the great taste of fries and ketchup. The problem is how to serve them in a dip yet keep the same flavors and textures. This recipe solves that problem by partially mashing the fries into ketchup. The basic ingredients are still recognizable, and even the hardest fries tend to get soggy enough to be in a dip. Serve with chips or pretzels.

4 cups	**French fries, leftover or freshly fried**
2 large bottles	**ketchup, cold**
2 tsp.	**salt**
1 tsp.	**soy sauce**
1 tsp.	**pepper**
1 squirt	**mustard (for garnish)**

1. Zap the fries in a microwave for 2 minutes until steamy. If the fries are old, sprinkle with water first to make them more soggy.
2. Chop the fries with a fork until they are half-mashed. Stir in the ketchup and all of the remaining ingredients, except the mustard.
3. Squirt on the mustard and serve immediately. It's like a hot fudge sundae—the heat of the fries and the cold of the ketchup are great together.

   SERVES: 4 TO 6

No-Op Dip

 For you non techies, a No-Op was an assembly-language statement used to fill space. In the old days of main-frames, it did nothing. Well, this dip is used to fill space. It has no cholesterol or fat and is practically tasteless. If there weren't the salt, you'd swear it was a mistake. It is designed to be served when you have fussy guests. (You know, the ones everyone else hates to be around because they can't eat anything you serve or they are on a diet, or whatever.) Point these people in the direction of this dip and you'll be sure to please them. Keep reminding them that it is fat-free, and they will ignore their taste buds. Have enough on hand for unannounced visits.

2 pounds	**unflavored gelatin**
1 cup	**leftover white rice (optional)**
dash	**salt**

1. Whip the gelatin until it looks like regurgitated agar. Mix in the rice and salt.
2. Store in the refrigerator (this dip will keep for months!)
3. Serve cold with celery.

   SERVES: 4 TO 6

Minced Burger Dip

 This dip is a great complement to Fries and Ketchup Dip (see page 34)—both give you that diner feeling. The trick is to cut up the burgers so that the buns adhere to the burgers themselves. Keep the patties in place by using old burgers where the ketchup has congealed onto the meat.

1 dozen	**day-old burgers with buns**
1 cup	**mayonnaise**
1 cup	**mustard or ketchup**
1/2 cup	**Worcestershire sauce**
1 tsp.	**salt**
1 tsp.	**pepper**

1. Zap the burgers for 2 minutes until the buns soften. Make sure you take the foil wrappers off first.
2. Put burgers on a clean counter and let cool. Chop them into bite-sized pieces.
3. Mix the remaining ingredients in a large bowl.
4. Stir in the chopped burgers.
5. Serve immediately.

   SERVES: 4 TO 6

Leftover Chinese Food Dip

Like many hackers, you may tire of Chinese food—especially when you've had it in your refrigerator for ages. The solution is to disguise it and serve it as a dip to guests. It tastes great, and most of your guests will feel as if they've visited a foreign country. Serve with chips, pretzels, or, for that special taste, tortillas.

2 cartons	leftover Chinese food
1 bottle	sweet and sour sauce
1 cup	mayonnaise
1 cup	crispy Chinese noodles
2 tbsp.	soy sauce
dash	salt
dash	pepper

1. Zap the Chinese food for about 2 minutes. Add a splash of water to the food if the rice is too dry.
2. Stir in the remaining ingredients.
3. Serve immediately.

SERVES: 4 TO 6

Engine Dip

This dip is meant to clean your rings! It is dark and spicy, but creamy. It is the perfect complement to a day tinkering with a favorite low-level driver. Serve with chips or warm tortillas.

2 cans	chili without beans
2 cups	soy sauce
1 cup	mayonnaise
1 cup	spicy (hot) salsa
2 cups	green chilies, chopped

1. Combine the ingredients in a large bowl.
2. Zap in a microwave for 2 minutes until steamy.
3. Serve immediately.

SERVES: 4 TO 6

Corn Salad Dip

There is nothing better than a large bowl of corn salad to start a meal. This popular substitute combines the flavors of corn salad with the ease of eating it in a dip.

4 large cans	corn
1 cup	mayonnaise
1/2 cup	soy sauce
1/2 cup	corn mush (optional)
8	corn tortillas, chopped
1 tbsp.	spicy (hot) salsa
1 cup	green chilies, chopped

1. Combine the ingredients in a large bowl.
2. Zap in a microwave for 1 minute until just warm. Be sure to watch the time—otherwise, the mayonnaise might separate.
3. Serve immediately.

SERVES: 4 TO 6

Whipped Pizza Dip

This creation started with leftover pizza, a large party, and no dips to serve. Under the pressure of time, the host whipped together—literally—a dip that was an instant hit. Use leftover or freshly made pizza for this dip. Pepperoni, mushroom, or anchovy pizza gives the best taste combination.

1 large	**pizza (preferably pepperoni, mushroom, or anchovy)**
1 small can	**sliced mushrooms**
1 can	**chopped olives**
1 cup	**mayonnaise**
1/2 cup	**ketchup**
1/2 cup	**soy sauce**
1 tsp.	**chili sauce**
dash	**salt**
dash	**pepper**

1. Chop the pizza into bite-sized pieces using a sharp knife.
2. Zap the pizza in a microwave until the cheese melts.
3. Combine pizza with the remaining ingredients in a large bowl. Whip until all the pieces of the pizza are submerged in the sauce.
4. Serve with chips, pretzels, or celery.

    SERVES: 4 TO 6

Hacker Guacamole

If you are serving Mexican food, some beer and a large bowl of guacamole will put your guests in the right frame of mind. Hacker Guacamole is spicy and chunky, combining the smoothness of the avocados with the crunchiness of leftover chips or pretzels. Most corner stores now carry premade guacamole, but any green-colored dip and mashed soft avocados can be substituted to give roughly the same taste.

2 tubs	**premade guacamole**
1/2 cup	**spicy (hot) salsa**
1 can	**whole olives**
1/2 cup	**mayonnaise**
1 cup	**leftover chips or pretzels**
dash	**salt**
dash	**pepper**

1. Combine the ingredients in a large bowl.
2. Stir until the mixture is smooth and chunky.
3. Serve with corn chips or warm tortillas.

    SERVES: 4 TO 6

Leftover Chip Dip

If you entertain often, you will regularly experience the problem of what to do with leftover chips and pretzels. Store them in a bag until you have enough to make this dip.

4 cups	**old chips**
1 can	**chopped olives**
1 packet	**onion dip**
1 cup	**sour cream**
1/2 cup	**ketchup**
1/2 cup	**spicy (hot) salsa**
dash	**salt**
dash	**pepper**

1. Combine the ingredients in a large bowl and let soak for 20 minutes or until chips soften. (If you cannot wait, then 5 minutes will do.)
2. Stir until the mixture is smooth and chunky.
3. Serve with chips.

SERVES: 4 TO 6

Cool Whip Dip

Next to the wheel, Cool Whip is humankind's greatest invention. Its smooth, creamy taste goes great with anything—from desserts to dips. This simple recipe clocks in under 1 minute to prepare and provides a sweet alternative to onion dip at a party. Put it out on the table with your other dips and watch the faces of your happy guests. Try serving this with chips or chocolate bars.

1 tub	**Cool Whip**
1/2 cup	**powdered sugar**
1 tsp.	**cinnamon**
dash	**salt**

1. Combine the ingredients in a large bowl. Whip until smooth.
2. Serve immediately.

SERVES: 4 TO 6

Bubba-ganush

This heavy-handed version of the Middle Eastern favorite babaganush (pronounced buh-buh-ga-nush) embell-ishes the base of charbroiled eggplants with a Mexican flavor. The recipe has been reduced to under 10 minutes and delivers the smoky taste we expect from Middle Eastern food.

1 packet	**babaganush mix**
1 to 2	**water (follow**
cups	**instructions on dip packet)**
1 can	**green chilies, chopped**
1 tbsp.	**salsa**
1 can	**chopped olives**
1/2 bottle	**Cheez Whiz**
1 tsp.	**garlic salt**
dash	**pepper**
1 package	**falafel bread or Ritz crackers**

1. Follow the directions on the babaganush mix packet. (To save you time, this recipe calls for mix. If you cannot find babaganush mix, use any other kind of quick dip mix. Hummus and onion soup mix are good substitutes.)

2. Fold in remaining ingredients and stir in a large bowl.
3. Serve with Ritz crackers or sliced falafel bread.

SERVES: 4 TO 6

Blazing Hummus Dip

This favorite Middle Eastern fare has been "hacked" with more spices and chunkier ingredients by some hackers who were unable to leave well enough alone.

1 packet	hummus mix
1 to 2 cups	water (follow instructions on dip packet)
1/2 cup	sour cream
1/2 can	garbanzo beans
3 to 6	jalapeño chilies, chopped
1 tbsp.	salsa
1 can	chopped olives
1/2 bottle	Cheez Whiz
1 tsp.	garlic salt
dash	pepper
1 package	falafel bread or Ritz crackers

1. Follow the directions on the hummus mix. (For variety, try substituting babaganush mix for the hummus mix.)
2. Fold in remaining ingredients and stir in a large bowl.
3. Serve with Ritz crackers or sliced falafel bread.

SERVES: 4 TO 6

Debugging and eating

One of the most challenging aspects of hackerdom is debugging. Searching out logical varmints takes all of a hacker's mental energy, and stoking the fire with a healthy dip is always beneficial. Keep food at the hottest spice level that you can endure to invigorate the senses. Always place the bowls within dipping distance and in large quantities.

Three-Bean Dip

If you are tired of those three-bean salads that seem to propagate in deli windows, this new twist will pleasantly surprise you. Three-Bean Dip actually has five types of beans suspended in sour cream and seasoned with horseradish. The blandness of the beans and the spiciness of the horseradish give this dip an unusual flavor. Serve with reinforced crackers.

1 can	pinto beans
1 can	garbanzo beans
1 can	kidney beans
1 can	lima beans
1 can	refried beans
1 cup	sour cream
2 tbsp.	vegetable oil

1 cup	horseradish
1 tsp.	Worcestershire sauce
dash	salt
dash	pepper

1. Combine the ingredients in a large bowl and stir until lumpy.
2. Serve immediately.

SERVES: 4 TO 6

Roughage Whip

This nutritious dish combines high-quality fiber with good taste in a dip that takes aim at the lower digestive tract. Serve the dip with plenty of water, and group catharsis will take on a special meaning.

1 can	sauerkraut
1 can	prunes, mashed
1 can	refried beans
1 cup	mayonnaise
2 tbsp.	vegetable oil
1 tsp.	sugar
dash	salt
dash	pepper

1. Combine the ingredients in a large bowl and stir until thick.
2. Serve immediately.

SERVES: 4 TO 6

Cold Gravy Dip

Congealed gravy is the most misunderstood food in the refrigerator. Although most people think it appears inedible until warmed, a few brave souls have pioneered serving leftover gravy straight from the refrigerator as a unique dip. The hardened fat on the top can be removed for the squeamish or dieters but alternatively adds a wonderful, slippery feel to the dip. Mix in corn and pinto beans, and you have a hearty meal, suitable for even the most meat-and-potatoes individuals among us.

2 cups	cold brown gravy
1 can	pinto beans
1 can	corn
1 small can	sliced mushrooms
1 tsp.	garlic salt
dash	salt
dash	pepper

1. Combine the ingredients in a large bowl. Stir until thick and lumpy.
2. Serve immediately.

SERVES: 2 TO 4

Dinners

The Coup de Grâce

DINNERS HAVE TRADITIONALLY been eaten at the end of long nights of hacking and served in the early morning hours just before dawn. This is when clusters of hackers would emerge from their labs and traipse over to the twenty-four-hour coffee shops. Out of the kitchens would roll hamburgers, fries, milkshakes, sundaes—anything and everything the chef had on hand from the dinner crowd the night before. If a hacker had a day job, he would try to squeeze in a couple of hours of sleep after his dinner before getting on his machine once again. For students, class would start.

In either case, dinner was a celebration. The sun was going to rise again and the night's efforts were completed, at least for the time being.

When the act of walking became too much of a distraction, dinners moved to the lab. The same celebratory air pervaded the entire meal. Soon the smells of cheese and meat would come waft-ing through the air as hackers stoked up their microwaves in makeshift kitchens alongside their computers. Old printouts would serve as cutting boards, slide rules as handy knives or spoons. Soon dinner would be warm enough and irresistible to the hungry and frenzied hackers in the room.

So hacker dinners were born.

The most notorious dinners to have their origins in the labs were the *leftover dinners*. Here the basic ingredient was a previous meal hidden at the back of a refrigerator. Where other cuisines might start with a roux or sauce, hacker fare started with what was left in the refrigerator. This culinary tradition kept expenses relatively low, although the first attempts were marked with reported cases of dysentery, chronic headaches, and yeast infections. Needless to say, this technique has come a long way from its origins, and today hackers find themselves in a higher income bracket. Such rummaging in public refrigerators is no longer necessary: Hackers' own refrigerators are a perfect source for old meals, and with better health care, most infections and maladies can be quickly treated with no lingering embarrassment or side effects.

Serving from Containers

In hacker mode, using the original or recycled containers to serve is de rigueur. Although modern tastes are leaning more toward ceramics, this original style of serving is experiencing a revival of sorts. For single-ingredient meals, simply remove the lid and serve the contents at room temperature.

For any large, complicated dishes, after you prepare the dish as required, return it to a large survival container. Make sure any sharp edges are removed from the opening. Pork and bean containers are highly desirable for this task, since they add a certain trough milieu to the meal.

These containers can be reused. Wipe clean with a soapy cloth, rinse and dry. Keep the labels dry.

The Art of the Leftover

There is an inside joke in the hacker community. Where other cuisines have recipes that have been handed down from generation to generation, hacker cuisine has actual meals handed down for generations. By nature, the hacker is not apt to throw much away.

After years of being reminded of the starving masses outside the borders of their country, hackers stow their leftovers in any container that can be appropriated for the purpose. (See Appendix A: The Zen of Cleaning Up.) A large take-out dinner may be placed into the refrigerator and recycled into another dish. This dish in turn may not be finished, so may in turn be shelved and recycled once again. In the end, the Chinese mushroom that was recycled into the original fried rice at your local take-out may surface years later in a Deadhead Breadball Casserole (page 44)—with a completely new color, texture, and taste. To a hacker, biting into this morsel can be a religious experience.

The secret to any dinner that incorporates leftovers is, of course, the knack of combining unique tastes. For timid chefs, mixing leftover spaghetti with old Jell-O may be too much. Yet in the hands of a seasoned hacker, these two foods—mixed with a little pepper and jalapeño—can be transformed into a fiery dip. The same hacker may instead infuse the mixture with a heavy dose of chocolate, brown sugar, and cinnamon and transmute it into a palatable dessert. This is sheer hacker alchemy! The key, of course, is imagination, and what seems to work best is the art of free association. One must clear one's mind and let the basic contents of the refrigerator dictate the recipe. A hacker at work assembling his leftovers most resembles a patient facing a psychiatrist: The inner recesses of the patient's mind (as represented by the refrigerator) are laid bare on the counter. The jumble of free association folds the ingredients into unlikely but pleasing configurations, and the result is a Rorschach blend of colors and shapes.

Rules of Thumb

There are a number of rules that, if followed, can produce a higher percentage of great tasting dishes.

- Combine older dishes with newer ones. Where ingredients in one set of leftovers may be too mushy, they will be offset by the relative crispness of newer ingredients.

- Always include some freshly opened ingredients. Too many leftovers in a dish will simply taste too old. There is no fooling the hacker palate. Add freshly opened cans to leftovers for great results.

- Diversity is the goal. There is nothing more boring than mixing similar dishes or textures together to form a new recipe. Although Michelangelo Lasagna Sandwiches (see page 55) have long been a favorite of hackers, you will get more mileage when you combine some Italian leftovers with Chinese or Lebanese leftovers. Or try combining chopped peanut butter sandwiches with bottom-of-the-bag chips or pretzels. Here the crispness of the chips brings out the mushiness of the peanut butter.

- Leftovers need not stand on their own. Although you may look at some leftovers and find their color or texture rather disappointing, keep in mind that you are not going to eat them by themselves. Their flavors will be mingled with those of other ingredients to produce unexpected new sensations. In much the same way that sourdough starter, with its frothy, unpleasant taste, is combined with a little flour and yeast and cooked to a golden brown, so this mixture of old and new can be quite wonderful.

- So do not let frothy, mildewed leftovers dissuade you from a final dish. These ingredients do not need to stand on their own. That they are capable of standing full height in your refrigerator—without the aid of a container—should not be unnerving.

- Thaw your leftovers first, then mix. As a rule, leftovers that have been left in the refrigerator or freezer will have melded together into a rigid, glutinous mass. Many older leftovers resemble the monolith in *2001*. Chinese leftovers may end up looking like cubed potting soil. As mentioned before, this should not deter you from using them in your meal.

■ Just be sure to thaw frozen leftovers before folding them into other ingredients. Do this by placing the leftovers into a microwave and zapping it for a short time. The congealed mass should loosen up enough to be separated into a bowl. Dishes that have a high grease level should return to their malleable liquid state.

■ Pick through your leftovers. You will be surprised what you will find. As long as an ingredient is edible, leave it alone. Discard any unusual but inedible elements.

With these simple guidelines, using leftovers can be a fun and highly enlightened practice. As always, the key is creativity.

Wonder Bread Balls

A unique accompaniment to any meal is a Wonder Bread Ball. To prepare, take a standard loaf of Wonder bread, compress all of the slices into one large ball, press down on a plate, and serve warm. The ball can be sliced for guests or simply torn for a casual meal.

Presto! Your mixture is once again in the bowl, and you are ready to move ahead.

Chinese Noodle Spaghetti

Tired of the same spaghetti every night? Then switch to Chinese crispy noodles, available in cans at the grocer's. Preparing this crunchy alternative is much quicker than cooking regular spaghetti and dresses up an otherwise normal meal.

2 cups	crispy Chinese noodles
1 jar	spaghetti sauce
2 tbsp.	chopped garlic
1 small can	sliced mushrooms
1 tsp.	garlic salt
dash	salt
dash	pepper

1. Submerge the noodles in a bowl of cold water for 5 minutes to ensure the desired soggy texture.
2. Combine the ingredients in a large bowl.
3. Stir until thick and lumpy.
4. Zap in a microwave for 5 minutes.
5. Serve immediately.

SERVES: 2 TO 4

Deadhead Breadball Casserole

This vintage sixties recipe has been updated to include more veggies, but it still has the unbeatable original

texture. It dates back to Grateful Dead dinners, where a filling casserole was the best cure for those preconcert munchies. Serve as a side dish at barbecues, a quick dinner, or a late night snack.

1 loaf	**Wonder bread or other soft white bread**
2	**eggs**
1 tsp.	**butter**
2 tsp.	**salt**
1 cup	**pre-grated cheddar cheese**
1 can	**new potatoes**
1 can	**cream of mushroom soup**
1 can	**creamed corn**
1/2 tsp.	**pepper**
1 cup	**bread crumbs**

1. Put bread on a clean counter or in a large bowl. Crack eggs over the top of the bread and mix thoroughly until the loaf is one large, sticky mass. Ball up single slices by cupping the bread between your hands and pressing tightly. For better presentation, poke the crusts into the center of each ball. Set aside. Wipe your hands on a clean dishtowel.

2. In a large saucepan, quickly melt the butter. Add the breadballs and sauté until they are browned on all sides. Stir gently or flip á la Galloping Gourmet.

3. Combine all of the remaining ingredients except the bread crumbs. Stir until mixture is hot and the cheese has melted completely. Add water if the mixture is too sticky.

4. Sprinkle the bread crumbs over the top and serve directly from the pan.

SERVES: 1 OR 2

Breadball Marinara

 A vegetarian alternative to meatballs, this classic dish is best after a full day of marinating. This popular variation is served often at Route 101 basement parties. Serve it with jug wine and loud music, and you've got a real celebration.

1 loaf	**Wonder bread or other soft white bread**
2	**eggs**
1 tsp.	**butter**
1 tsp.	**mashed garlic**
1 jar	**Newman's Own Sockarooni spaghetti sauce**
1/2 tsp.	**pepper**
2 tsp.	**salt**
1 tsp.	**Parmesan cheese**

1. Make breadballs for Deadhead Breadball Casserole (see page 44).

2. In a saucepan, quickly melt the butter. Add the breadballs and garlic and sauté until browned on all sides. Stir gently.

3. Empty the jar of spaghetti sauce into the pan, stirring carefully around the breadballs until all of the sauce is hot and the breadballs are

warm to the touch. Add remaining ingredients. Avoid overcooking.

4. Pour over leftover spaghetti or toast. Sprinkle the cheese just before serving.

SERVES: 1 OR 2

Variations:

Breadball Marinara and Spaghettios. Pour the mixture over a bowl of Spaghettios, and you have a quick lunch or side dish.

Breadball Marinara on Toasted Bagel. Pour the mixture over a toasted sesame bagel, and you will have a great surprise. Although this Jewish-Italian combination is a little on the heavy side, it can be a great breakfast meal after a night of NoDoz.

Breadball Marinara Sandwich. Place a row of breadballs in a hot dog bun or Italian roll for a great lunch treat.

Pretzel knee squats

The secret to pouring pretzels or chips from a bag is making sure that they are in small pieces so they flow smoothly. Hackers have come up with a technique that both opens the bag and crushes the pretzels inside:

1. Place the unopened bag of pretzels behind both knees.
2. In one fast motion, do a deep knee squat. Your weight should come directly down on the bag with a loud pop.

The bag is ready for pouring. Not only will this open the bag and crush the pretzels inside, but it will clear out the kitchen of any rodents.

Pretzel Lasagna

Pretzel lasagna solves the classic problem of what to eat when you are dying for some good Italian food and can't wait another second for the noodles to boil. By substituting pretzels (or other variants; see below), you can achieve a great approximation. For less crunchy lasagna, put the pretzels in a bowl of milk and zap it for 4 minutes in the microwave.

1 tsp.	**butter**
1/2 bag	**salted pretzels**
1 can	**stewed tomatoes (if you like tomatoes)**
3 tsp.	**mashed garlic**
1 jar	**Newman's Own Sockarooni spaghetti sauce**

1 jar	Cheez Whiz (or 5 inches of Velveeta)
2 tsp.	salt
1 tsp.	Parmesan cheese
1/2 tsp.	pepper

1. In a saucepan, bring the butter to a quick melt and throw in pretzels and garlic until they are lightly coated on all sides. Stir gently to avoid crushing the pretzels.
2. Pour the spaghetti sauce, stewed tomatoes, and Cheez Whiz into the pan, stirring until bubbling and lumpy. Add salt to taste.
3. Set aside and let cool. Shake pepper and Parmesan cheese on top of lasagna before serving.

SERVES: 1 OR 2

Variations:

Pretzel Lasagna with Macaroni and Cheese. This is a leftover dish, combining leftover macaroni and cheese with the Pretzel Lasagna. Cut the Cheez Whiz by half unless you are a real cheezaholic.

Potato Chip Lasagna. Follow the basic recipe but use nearly a full bag of potato chips instead of pretzels. Stir very carefully to avoid unnecessary breakage.

Slim Jim Lasagna. Using either pretzel or potato chip "pasta," add chopped Slim Jims for a beefy taste.

Chinese Leftovers Lasagna

After a few too many dog days of Chinese leftovers, you may still have more remaining. Disguise it by stirring it into the basic Pretzel Lasagna. You will no longer recognize the nationality (avoid egg rolls or soup to preserve the delicate taste of this special dish).

1 tsp.	butter
1/2 bag	salted pretzels
1 can	stewed tomatoes (if you like tomatoes)
3 tsp.	mashed garlic
1 jar	Newman's Own Sockarooni spaghetti sauce
1 jar	Cheez Whiz (or 5 inches of Velveeta)
2 tsp.	salt
1 carton	Chinese leftovers
1 tsp.	Parmesan cheese
1/2 tsp.	pepper

1. Prepare the basic Pretzel Lasagna recipe (see page 46).
3. Stir the carton of Chinese leftovers in with the spaghetti sauce (leave out the rice unless you need added bulk). Add the tomatoes and simmer.
4. Shake pepper and Parmesan cheese on top of lasagna before serving.

SERVES: 1 OR 2

Mashed Potato Chips

 This quick recipe is a great crowd pleaser. The crunchy texture of the chips and the smooth feel of the instant potatoes will delight even the most "had-it-all" hackers.

1 box	**instant potatoes (optional)**
1 bag	**plain potato chips**
1 cup	**milk (or substitute sour cream for a great taste!)**
1 tsp.	**Parmesan cheese**
1/2 tsp.	**pepper**
1 tsp.	**salt**
1 tsp.	**mashed garlic**
2 tsp.	**butter**
1/2 tsp.	**paprika (optional)**
1/2 cup	**chopped olives (optional)**

1. (Optional) In a large saucepan, stir in the instant potatoes, following the directions on the side of the box. Substituting milk wherever water is mentioned in the recipe for this will give a smoother texture. Make sure there is enough room in the pan for the potato chips.
2. In a large bowl, dump as much of the bag of chips as you can. With a fork (or potato masher, if you are so endowed), mash the chips while pouring the milk over the top. Add remaining ingredients. Zap in the microwave for 3 minutes until the corners of the chips are less ragged. (Alternatively, pour the milk into the bag and zap.)
3. Fold into the instant potatoes and stir until lumpy. Add the Parmesan cheese and pepper.
4. Set aside and let cool. Shake paprika on top or add some olives for garnish.

SERVES: 1 OR 2

Variations:

Mashed Potato Chips au Gratin. Just before you remove the potatoes from the stove, stir in a small jar of Cheez Whiz. Let it swirl. Before serving, sprinkle the top with large cubes of Velveeta.

Mashed French Fries. Zap a half bag of frozen French fries until room temperature, then mash and add to the instant potatoes. This substitute is not quite as crunchy or tasty as the original, but some hackers prefer it.

Mashed Spaghetti

 This recipe originated when leftover spaghetti was inadvertently mixed incorrectly in a bowl, resulting in the pasty consistency that hackers enjoy. Mixed with your favorite spaghetti sauce, this dish can be surprisingly satisfying as a side dish or a meal unto itself.

1 pound	**cooked spaghetti**
1 jar	**spaghetti sauce**
1 cup	**Parmesan cheese**
1 tsp.	**salt**
1/2 tsp.	**pepper**

1. Mash the spaghetti in a large bowl. Dump in the spaghetti sauce, cheese, salt, and pepper, and stir thoroughly.
2. Zap for two minutes and serve immediately.

SERVES: 1 OR 2

Potato Dogs

 The Earl of Sandwich has nothing on this new hot dog bun: It's a hollowed-out potato that's as much fun for the hackers in your family as it is for the preschoolers. To avoid accidents, let the Potato Dogs cool after they come out of the microwave!

6   long raw potatoes

6   hot dogs (match the lengths of the hot dogs to the lengths of the potatoes)

1. Scrub the potatoes with a scouring pad—remember, there are chemicals, pesticides, and fingernail grunge in unwashed potato skins. Cut off any blemishes.
2. With a steak knife or pocket knife, core the potatoes lengthwise. The opening in each should be a little over an inch in diameter—about the thickness of your hot dogs. Poke the potatoes several times with a fork.
3. Zap each potato for 3 minutes to precook. Turn over and zap again for another 3 minutes.
4. Remove the potatoes and let cool. Unwrap the hot dogs and stab each several times with a fork.

5. Stuff one hot dog into each potato, using a paper towel to protect your hands from the heat. Set aside.
6. Zap each stuffed potato for 2 minutes more or until the ends of the hot dogs pop. Do not overcook.
7. Let the Potato Dogs cool about 5 minutes before serving. Squirt with mustard or ketchup to taste.

SERVES: 3 TO 6

Variation:

Potato Dogs au Gratin. During their last 30 seconds in the microwave, top Potato Dogs with Cheez Whiz for extra great taste!

Fish Stick Stir-fry

 The problem with frozen fish sticks is that they usually taste like cardboard. The batter helps, of course, but after a number of days in the refrigerator, they need some pizzazz. Fish Stick Stir-Fry combines fish sticks with a cheesy mushroom sauce for an interesting change of pace.

1 box	**frozen fish sticks**
1 tsp.	**butter**
1 jar	**Cheez Whiz**
1 can	**cream of mushroom soup**
1 can	**corn**
1 small can	**chopped olives**

1 small can	sliced mushrooms
1 cup	bread crumbs
1/2 tsp.	pepper
1/2 tsp.	salt

1. Zap the fish sticks until room temperature.
2. In a saucepan, melt the butter and add the fish sticks. Stir until all sticks are coated with the butter. Do not worry about breaking the pieces. This is a natural consequence of cooking and contributes to the presentation of this dish. Your friends may never guess that they are eating fish sticks! To enhance texture, mash the fish sticks with a fork.
3. Add remaining ingredients and bring to a simmer. Remove from heat and serve warm.

SERVES: 2 TO 4

Fish Stick Niçoise

This dish takes its name from the French classic salad niçoise, which combines potatoes, tuna fish, and salad fixings. Substitute crispy Chinese noodles for lettuce if you're not a veggie eater.

1 box	frozen fish sticks
5 inches	Velveeta cheese
1/2 can	lima beans
1/2 can	garbanzo beans
1/2 can	new potatoes

1 small can	sliced mushrooms
1 handful	corn
dash	chopped olives
1 handful	lettuce, torn up
dash	pepper
dash	salt
1/2 cup	Italian salad dressing

1. Zap the fish sticks for about 1 minute. They should still be cold.
2. Cut the cheese into large cubes about 1 inch wide.
3. In a large bowl, combine all of the remaining ingredients except the salad dressing and toss gently. Sprinkle the salad dressing over the top to taste.

SERVES: 2 TO 4

Hot-dog Stroganoff

You aren't likely to find this classic knock-off at any respectable restaurant. You will be hard pressed to distinguish the original from this savory dish, which combines the creamy texture and taste of a good beef stew with the convenience of hot-dogs. The key is the sauce, which covers up almost any meat—the thicker, the better.

1 tbsp.	butter
2 tsp.	mashed garlic
1 package	hot dogs

1 packet	instant brown sauce
1 can	cream of mushroom soup
1 cup	milk
1 can	peas
1 small can	sliced mushrooms
1/2 small jar	Cheez Whiz
1/2 cup	bread crumbs
1 can	new potatoes
1 handful	black olives, chopped
dash	pepper
1/2 tsp.	salt

1. In a large saucepan, melt the butter with the garlic. Cut the hot dogs into 1-inch sections and toss into the saucepan. Brown on all sides for about 2 minutes.
2. Add the instant brown sauce, the cream of mushroom soup, and the milk. Bring to a simmer.
3. Add the remaining ingredients and let boil until gooey.
4. Serve over toast, leftover rice, or noodles or by itself if you are in a rush.

SERVES: 2 TO 4

Variations:

Bologna or Spam Stroganoff. Substitute Spam or bologna cut into strips for the hot dogs.

Leftover Burger Stroganoff. If you have burgers left over from a previous meal, chop them up, bun and all, and substitute for the hot dogs.

Oinkers

For you pork lovers, Oinkers can't be beat. The name comes from the mind numbing Roll-the-Pigs game, which can be played ad nauseam on airplanes, between sets or compiles, or after a heavy night of drinking. Oinkers are the perfect snack—heavy on the pork, light on the carbs.

1 large can	deviled ham
1 tsp.	mashed garlic
dash	soy sauce
1 tsp.	salt

Wonder Bread Pen Holder

An unexpected outcome of the Wonder Bread Ball (see page 44) is the Wonder Bread Pen Holder, made from the semirigid leftovers of an evening meal. Although the balls themselves can be kept indefinitely, there comes a time when one risks dental work in eating them. When rigor mortis sets in, it is best to find other uses for the bread. A pen holder is ideal, especially alongside the computer.

dash	pepper
1/2 cup	bread crumbs
6 slices	Wonder or other soft white bread
1 can	Vienna sausage
1 can	Canadian bacon
1/2 cup	mayonnaise

1. In a bowl, mix the deviled ham, garlic, soy sauce, salt, pepper, and bread crumbs. The resulting mixture should be thick and sticky. Arrange three slices of the bread on a plate and spread the mixture over each, about 1″ thick, until all of the mixture is used up.

2. Open the sausage and Canadian bacon. Lay a slice of bacon on each piece of bread (on top of the mixture), then a few sausages, and finally any remaining bacon. The mixture should bind the ingredients so that none of the bacon or sausage shakes loose.

3. Zap the assembly in the microwave for about 1 to 2 minutes to warm up the mixture. Spread each remaining slice of bread with mayonnaise and place on top of the bottom pieces. Serve with chips and Cokes.

SERVES: 2 OR 3

Variations:

Spam Oinkers. Mash Spam in a small bowl in place of the deviled ham. Use some mayonnaise to hold it together.

Oinker Boinkers. Add thick slices of Velveeta

and pimentos before you microwave for a great cheesy flavor.

Jalapeño Oinkers. Add a dash of Tabasco and some jalapeño peppers for a south-of-the-border bite.

Hacker Subs

Originally sandwiches were invented with the hacker in mind. Although the size of the typical hacker sandwich is large in comparison with its non-hacker counterpart, deli food is the lifeblood of any hacker's diet. It can be eaten while working without messing up the keyboard and keeps in a refrigerator for long periods.

1 tsp.	mustard (optional)
1 12-inch	bread roll, cut in half
2 packages	deli turkey
1/2 pound	salami
1/2 pound	cheddar cheese
2 tbsp.	chopped olives
2 tbsp.	green chilies, chopped
1 leaf	lettuce (optional)
1/4 cup	mayonnaise
dash	pepper
dash	salt

1. Spread the mustard on the bottom of one half of the bread roll. Pile the dry ingredients on top. Spoon the mayonnaise on top of the meats, sprinkle with pepper and salt, and place the remaining half of the roll on top.

2. Press down firmly until the sandwich looks as if it will fit in a person's mouth.
3. Serve immediately with potato salad and chips.

SERVES: 2 OR 3

Variations:

Spaghetti Sub. Use leftover spaghetti with sauce in place of the meats.

Leftover Chinese Food Sub. Use leftover Chinese food as the main ingredient. Make sure the rice is soft before assembling the sandwich.

Spam Trotters

Bean dip-based Spam Trotters are aptly named for their high fiber content, especially when you add prunes. For obvious reasons, really good bean dips have always had a cathartic effect on people. The best bean dips are very spicy, jammed with thick bean mash, and packed with soft whole beans. We recommend reconstituting commercially available bean dips with canned beans, corn flakes (for a little crunch), and chili peppers (for the added punch).

1 large can	**Spam**
1 large can	**bean dip**
1 tsp.	**mashed garlic**
1/2 jar	**Cheez Whiz**

Laxatives

More often than not, hackers do not need this remedy.

Yet there are times you may be stuck in unfamiliar territory. Take the case of Troy K., an unrepentant hacker who spent the summer with the Garcia family in the outreaches of Sonora. At their humble ranch, the family ate simple meals of tortillas, beans, and chilies. Although Troy took immediately to his favorite foods, tortillas and beans, he could not tolerate the fiery hot chilies. It was only after days of pure torture, when his bowels locked up like a old engine, that Troy finally sampled a roasted chili. He experienced what can only be described as nirvana. The ceramics of most toilet bowls are not equipped to handle the blast that shook the Garcia house that day.

Sadly, Mr. Garcia was the first to arrive at the scene, rifle in hand. He found Troy, pants at his ankles, smile on his face. Troy was one with the universe. He died a chili lover.

Some words of advice:
- Beans by themselves cannot keep you regular. Load up with an extra spoonful of bacon grease or teaspoon of hot chilies.
- In a bind, try a batch of Roughage Whip (see page 40).

1/2 cup	mayonnaise
3	jalapeño chilies
1 small can	chopped olives
dash	soy sauce
dash	pepper
1 can	pinto beans
1/2 cup	corn flakes

1. In a large bowl, mix all the ingredients except the beans and corn flakes.
2. Using a fork or potato masher, mash the beans and corn flakes until chunky. Stir them into mixed ingredients.
3. Spread on corn chips as an appetizer or over corn tortillas as a full meal.

SERVES: 2 OR 3

Variations:

Prune Trotters. Mash a handful of prunes in a small bowl, then add the other ingredients. The fiber content goes ballistic, but you add a rich, sweet flavor to the mix.

Sauerkraut Biscuits

One of the nicest, most heartwarming side dishes is hot biscuits. Betty Crocker and others have blazed the easy-to-make biscuit trail, and with a little practice, you can produce these in the microwave. The cup of sauerkraut and splash of beer give the biscuits a distinctively German accent. These biscuits are great for Oktoberfest or Unification drinking parties.

1 tin	buttermilk biscuits
1 cup	sauerkraut
1 tbsp.	soy sauce
1 splash	stale beer
1/2 tsp.	butter
dash	pepper

1. Slam the biscuit tin on the counter until the paper seams burst. Separate the biscuits onto your serving plate.
2. With your thumb and forefinger, stuff 1 teaspoon of sauerkraut inside each biscuit. Seal the bottom of each biscuit by pinching the raw dough together. Make sure the biscuit bottoms are down on the plate, or else the seams will show when you serve the biscuits.
3. Mix the soy sauce and beer together until light brown. Using a paper towel, coat the tops of the biscuits with this mixture. (This will make the biscuits look like they have been browned in a normal oven.)
4. Prick each biscuit on top with a fork; otherwise, they will explode in the microwave.
5. Zap for 8 to 10 minutes in a microwave (or as instructed on the biscuit label).
6. Serve hot with butter.

SERVES: 2 OR 3

Variations:

Potato Chip Biscuits. Mash a handful of potato chips in a small bowl and substitute them for the sauerkraut. Sprinkle some potato chip crumbs on top of the biscuits for garnish.

Popcorn Frittata

 This morning-after-the-movies dish uses leftover popcorn for an early morning wake-up meal.

2 tbsp.	butter
1 to 2 cups	popcorn
4	eggs
1/2 cup	milk (optional)
1 can	new potatoes, sliced
1 jar	Cheez Whiz
1 can	sliced mushrooms
1 can	Spam, diced
1 can	chopped olives
1 tsp.	soy sauce
dash	pepper
dash	salt

1. In a frying pan, melt the butter, then pour in the popcorn. Stir until the popcorn is evenly coated.
2. Beat the eggs, add them to the frying pan, and then add the remaining ingredients.
3. Stir frequently until slightly runny, then turn out in a serving dish.

SERVES: 2 OR 3

Michelangelo Lasagna Sandwich

 This hearty sandwich is rumored to have fueled Michelangelo's painting of the Sistine Chapel. His fondness for long work hours, cramped quarters, and unusual working positions have led many in the hacker community to consider Michelangelo one of the first hackers. This sandwich can be served on cold, rainy days or as an appetizer before a more filling main course. It is the ideal follow-up dish to Chinese Leftover Lasagna (page 47).

4	large rolls or submarine buns
2 pounds	leftover lasagna
1 tsp	soy sauce
1/2 pound	shredded Mozzarella cheese
2 tsp.	mashed garlic
1 jar	Cheez Whiz (or 5 inches of Velveeta)
1/2 tsp.	pepper
dash	salt (to taste)
1 tsp.	Parmesan cheese

1. Slice the rolls lengthwise and pile in the lasagna. Squeeze as much lasagna as you can into the rolls.
2. Over the tops of the rolls, layer the remaining ingredients.
3. Zap the sandwiches until steaming.

4. Shake pepper, salt, and Parmesan cheese on top before serving.

SERVES: 1 OR 2

Variations:

Spaghetti Sandwich. Substitute spaghetti for the lasagna.

Bean Barrel Sandwich. Substitute Bean Barrel (see page 27) for the lasagna.

Leftover Bean Dip Meatloaf

Having a hard time deciding whether to throw away soggy chips and old bean dip? This Leftover Bean Dip Meatloaf is the solution. It is easy to make and can be ready in a microwave in under 10 minutes.

1/2 cup	corn flakes
4	eggs
1 1/2 pounds	ground meat (optional)
1 can	whole mushrooms
1 can	chopped olives
2 tbsp.	butter
1 tsp.	soy sauce
dash	pepper
dash	salt
1 to 2 cups	leftover bean dip
1/2 cup	chips (optional)

1. On a microwavable plate, combine all of the ingredients except the bean dip and chips. Mold the mixture into a loaf. If the mixture does not stand up, add more corn flakes or use a bowl. Wipe your hands frequently to avoid sticking.
2. In a separate bowl, combine the bean dip and chips. Mash until chunky.
3. Using a large spoon or your fingers, press the bean mixture into the middle of the loaf, as if you are hiding it. Seal up the loaf and set it aside to rest a minute. (If you are not tired, you can continue.)
4. Zap the loaf for about 10 minutes, until the meat changes color. The loaf should be firm and hot to the touch.
5. Remove from the oven and let cool.

SERVES: 2 OR 3

Soggy Chips

If you live in a humid climate, your chips may get soggy quickly. The best solution is to eat the full bag, since any leftovers will deteriorate quickly.

Failing this, close up your bags and store them in the freezer. This will keep those chips in suspended animation for a long time. Even if the chips end up soggy, the freezing temperature will simulate the crunch that you like.

Variations:

Leftover Burger Meatloaf. Recycle those old burgers. Cut them up (bun and all) into 1-inch strips. Tuck inside the loaf instead of the bean mixture.

Chinese Leftover Meatloaf. Substitute leftover Chinese food for the bean mixture inside the loaf.

Breakfast Cheetos

 Although this classic is not a dinner, it is a great morning food that is noisy and filling. It is especially good with any leftovers in the fridge and a hot cup of coffee.

2 bags	Cheetos cheese snacks
2 jars	Cheez Whiz (optional)
1 tsp.	soy sauce
1 tsp.	pepper
1 squirt	mustard (for garnish)

1. Empty the Cheetos in a large bowl and cover with the remainder of the ingredients, except the mustard.
2. Zap lightly.
3. Squirt on the mustard and serve.

   SERVES: 4 TO 6

Horseradish Rice Balls

 Free white rice is the bane of most hackers because it piles up in the refrigerator and gets hard. This dish rejuvenates leftover rice and mixes in the spiciness of horseradish to cover over the musty refrigerator taste. Perfect for an after-Passover meal (with left-over "bitter herbs"), Horseradish Rice Balls can be substituted for Swedish meatballs or used with spaghetti.

3 sprinkles	water
2 cups	leftover rice
1/4 cup	white horseradish
1/2 cup	corn flakes
1	egg
1 tsp.	soy sauce
dash	pepper
dash	salt
4 tbsp.	butter

1. Mix the water with the rice, and zap lightly until the rice is soft. If this does not happen within 5 minutes, your rice is too old. Better put it back in the refrigerator as a baking soda deodorant. Switch to breadballs. (See variations below.)
2. In a separate bowl, combine all remaining ingredients except the butter. Mix thoroughly.
3. On high heat, melt butter in a large frying pan.
4. Roll the mixture into small balls or, if you are in a hurry, scoop with a small ice cream scoop. Drop balls into the frying pan. Roll around (the rice balls, that is) in the butter until brown on all sides.
5. Remove from the pan and serve immediately.

   SERVES: 2 OR 3

Variations:

Horseradish Breadballs. This is the same recipe except that the basic ingredient is bread. Roll the white bread into small balls, dunk around in the mixture above, and fry as directed.

Red Horseradish Rice Balls. Use red instead of white horseradish. Great for parties!

Five-Minute Burgers

The best Five-Minute Burgers are at your local hamburger drive-through. The basic directions are to order your burgers in advance and have them held under a fictitious name, which enables you to stop at another spot if you simply cannot hold out a second longer. Most drive-through establishments have wised up to this trick. (Don't worry about the burgers; after an hour they will be put with the rest.)

Alternatively, you may want to pull out the leftover burgers in your refrigerator and warm them in the microwave (not too long, or else they will become brittle).

As a last resort, the following recipe for Five-Minute Burgers is good.

4 patties	**precooked hamburger**
4 slices	**American cheese (optional)**
4 slices	**white bread (or 2 hamburger buns if you are lucky)**
1 tsp.	**ketchup or mustard**
1 tbsp.	**chopped onions**
2 tbsp.	**pickle slices**
2 tbsp.	**Thousand Island dressing (optional)**
1 tsp.	**soy sauce**
dash	**pepper**
dash	**salt**

1. Zap the hamburger patties until they are warm (make sure that these are the precooked variety—they should be dark hamburger color, not pink). Add the cheese for cheeseburgers, if you like.

2. Make two sandwiches by placing the patties on the bottom piece of bread or bun and piling the fixings on top. Add the Thousand Island dressing as secret sauce if you like.

SERVES: 1

Variations:

Fifteen-Minute Burgers. If your hamburger is pink in color, you'll need to cook it first. Get out the frying pan and cook 6 minutes per side, or until the pan smokes. (This type of cooking is a waste of time, so invest in some precooked patties to keep in your freezer.)

Five-Minute Fish Burgers. Substitute fish sticks for the meat. It's a great crowd pleaser if people notice the difference. Use tartar sauce instead of the dressing.

French Fries and Ketchup

 French fries are usually not considered a main course. However, they stand on their own alongside many of the more popular main courses (if they are physically standing up, something may be alive in those fries, so check before serving). The best fries are fresh from your local burger stand—the more oil the better. However, many stores now carry frozen fries. Choose the microwavable ones that require no browning.

4 cups	prefried French fries
1 cup	ketchup
dash	pepper
dash	salt

1. Zap the fries until steamy.
2. Load into a big bowl and pour the ketchup over the top. Sprinkle with salt. Serve immediately.

SERVES: 2 OR 3

Variations:

French Fries and Ketchup Soup. This variation has more ketchup than fries. Triple the ketchup and watch the fries swim.

Mashed French Fries and Ketchup. Although this variation can be made fresh, it usually works better with leftover French Fries and Ketchup Soup. Use a fork to mash your mixture. Serve warm.

Canned Soup

 This classic recipe was legitimized by the Space Age Cafe in Gila Bend, Arizona. When asked what the soup of the day was, the waitress would simply point to the row of cans on the top of the counter. They were displayed like dry cereal, and customers could choose the soup they wanted. Nothing beats a great can of soup. Why make it fresh when you can get it quick? The trick is not to add very much water.

2 cans	soup
water	(to taste)
1 tsp.	soy sauce
dash	pepper
dash	salt
1/2 cup	saltines, whole or pieces

1. Turn out the soup into a large bowl. Stir in the water until the soup loses its can shape. Add all remaining ingredients except the saltines.
2. Zap until warm. Stir and zap again.
3. Crumble in the saltines. Add more saltines if you want more of a "stew" consistency.
4. Serve immediately.

SERVES: 1

Variation:

Packaged Soup. Packaged soup is much too watery. However, in a bind, mix with sour cream and scoop.

Scraping

It is unfortunate that scraping has such a poor connotation in our society. Once a practice that was perfected in primitive cultures, it has fallen into disuse today, and millions of people neglect that last morsel of food at the bottom of cans and jars.

By all estimates, we waste 2 to 3 percent of our food by failing to scrape adequately. An extra second or two to scrape that remaining bit of food is all that it takes. Some guidelines:

- Reverse your spoon and use the handle to reach those crannies where the excess food resides.
- Rinse the can or jar with other ingredients to coax out these remaining morsels.
- At the end of the meal, squeegee your serving bowls with leftover bread or finger food.
- Do not use your fingers! The number of patients now admitted to emergency clinics with cans or jars stuck to their extremities continues to increase at an alarming rate.

Macaroni and Beef Jerky Casserole

 Although beef jerky was originally created to preserve meat from the elements, it has since found its way into classic hacker cuisine. Use small pieces and keep away from geriatrics and five- to eight-year-olds, among whom it's known as Loose Tooth Surprise. Easy to make and filling, this dish has long been a favorite of the Tex-Mex crowd as a break from standard just-north-of-the-border fare.

2 cans	macaroni and cheese
1/2 pound	beef jerky
1/2 cup	chopped olives
1/2 cup	chopped green chilies
1 tsp.	mustard (optional)
dash	pepper
dash	salt
1 cup	bread crumbs or corn flakes

1. Open and zap the canned macaroni and cheese.
2. With a large knife or meat cleaver, chop up the beef jerky into 1-inch squares. Soak in a little warm water to soften up.
3. In a large bowl, combine the beef jerky with the macaroni and cheese. Add the remaining ingredients, reserving a handful of bread crumbs for garnish.
4. Sprinkle the remaining bread crumbs on top.
5. Serve warm.

SERVES: 2 OR 3

Variations:

Macaroni and Slim Jim Casserole. Substitute Slim Jims for the beef jerky. You do not need to soften them first.

Macaroni and Vienna Sausage Casserole. Use 3 or 4 small cans of Vienna sausages instead of the beef jerky.

Five-Minute Pizza

There is no reason to make your own pizza. The key to this dish is timing. When should you call your favorite pizza delivery place? Before leaving work or about 45 minutes before you become ravenous, call for your pizza delivery. Always order as much pizza as you can fit in your refrigerator, because leftover pizza, whether warm, cold, or room temperature, is not half bad.

1   phone

1. Dial your local pizza delivery.
2. Pay the pizza person and eat.

SERVES: 2 OR 3

Spam Sushi

A local favorite on the island of Hawaii, this dish is a break from the raw fare normally pawned off as a delicacy. As with any Japanese sushi, the key is how the Spam is cut. The jellied consistency natu-

rally lends itself to being cut evenly and thickly. Spam Sushi hacker style quadruples the average serving size to make it resemble more of a rice sandwich than an appetizer. Comparing the average Japanese appetite with a hacker's should explain this fundamental variation.

1 carton	**leftover white rice**
2 cans	**Spam**
1/2 cup	**mayonnaise**
3 feet	**clean string (optional)**
dash	**salt**
1/4 cup	**soy sauce**

1. Splash water on the leftover rice and zap in the microwave until the rice softens. Do not heat the rice, since this dish is basically meant to be served cold. Chill the rice in the freezer while you prepare the Spam.
2. Turn out the Spam on a cutting board. Dampen your knife and slice the meat into 1-inch slices.
3. Pat the rice into paddies about the size of hamburger buns. Sushi is, after all, the Japanese equivalent of burgers. If the rice does not stick together, add mayonnaise.
4. Take one slice of Spam and one mound of rice. Dunk your forefinger into the mayonnaise and give your rice a quick streak of it, followed by a shake of salt (this is the equivalent of wasabi) before laying the meat on top. Carefully move it to a plate. If the Spam does not stay on top, use about 6 inches of string to tie it down.

5. Serve cold with soy sauce and French fries. Cut with a fork, then dunk in a communal bowl of soy sauce before eating.

   SERVES: 2 OR 3

Variations:

Tuna Fish Sushi. Place two large scoops of tuna fish salad instead of Spam on top of the rice.

Macaroni Sushi. Use chopped macaroni instead of the Spam for another taste sensation.

Spam Soup

This hearty soup is a quick variation of beef stew, without the beef, vegetables, and, some say, the taste, but it stands on its own as a classic hacker meal for cold days. Working the mound with a spoon will make it at least sit down.

2 cans	Spam, chopped
1 large jar	Cheez Whiz (optional)
1/2 can	chicken stock
1/2 can	cream of mushroom soup
dash	salt
dash	black pepper

1. Combine all of the ingredients in a large bowl. Make sure that your Spam is chopped.
2. With a fork or potato masher, knead the mixture into a thick, souplike consistency.
3. Zap in the microwave for about 3 minutes.
4. Serve hot with crackers.

   SERVES: 2 OR 3

Drinks

ALTHOUGH SEVERAL OF the recipes in this section are for alcoholic or sweet drinks, it is the caffeine drinks that go to the core of a hacker's existence. While it is not uncommon to see a hacker resting with a bottle of the local brew in hand, it is more common to see him bent over a screen with a Hammerhead—a highly potent caffeine blend of espresso, coffee, and powdered instant. This is the type of drink that a hacker craves, especially while in hack mode. Without caffeine, a hacker finds himself plodding along without his supercharge. Caffeine effectively cranks his clock speed.

Throughout the day, you will find some sort of caffeine drink set alongside a hacker's computer: a large sports bottle of Mountain Dew or mug of coffee or espresso. Life on the information highway is an accelerated journey in which time compresses and the hacker instincts must be honed to the nanosecond.

In short, you will usually see a hacker in one state—wired—and his drinks of choice while he's working always contain high levels of caffeine.

Getting Wired

There is simply too much to do these days—way too much! Leaving aside the technical journals and weekly news rags, there is just too much music, too many channels, and not enough time. There's more than can be crammed into a single day, at least at normal speed.

Caffeine is the only way to deal with it all—to cram more living into each day—more hacking, more CDs, more television, more music—much more of everything. The end of this century must be taken at high velocity, and getting frenzied is an easy, sustainable way to ride through some of the greatest experiences we will ever have. When the forests are gone and most animals are in zoos, life is going to be bleak, so now is the time to see it all and do it all.

Taking Off

Just how much caffeine you can tolerate is really up to you. Most users will disagree on how much is optimal: Some say that your speech should rat-

Caffeine States		
STATE	COFFEE LEVEL	DESCRIPTION
Taking off	1 cup	Eyes open; heart beating at 10 percent over norm.
Buzzing	2 cups	Lightheadedness; ability to think quickly (though not always clearly).
Flying	2 cups +	Heartbeat over 20 percent of norm; blitzing begins to happen; major bursts of creativity and energy.
Mach 2	3 cups	Speech reaches twice normal rates; REM may set in; hyperventilation may occur spontaneously. (Watch out!)
Mach 3	3 cups +	Internal dialogues whiz out of control; normal talking as we know it ceases; rapid-fire galactic insights occur; finger dexterity reaches peak levels.
Frenzied	4 cups +	The natural order of the world ceases to exist; user cannot do things quickly enough; "less is more" is taken to its limits; monosyllabic grunts are very common.

*COFFEE LEVEL IS BASED ON AN AVERAGE BODY WEIGHT OF 160 POUNDS.

tle at around Mach 2 (that is, twice your normal cadence). Others maintain that you should hit Mach 3 with your internal dialogue, and your rapid eye movements (REMs) should be nearly hypnotic. Almost everyone agrees, however, that your hands should remain free of jitters. It is a delicate balance.

Hackers love to maintain this so-called peak sailing while hacking. Caffeine facilitates *streaming*: time simply disappears because new ideas come so fast. One minute a hacker may be plugging away at a modest solution; the next moment that hacker is racing down the wind tunnel at the end of the movie *2001*, fingers madly trying to catch up with the brain as an elegant solution emerges from nowhere.

Keep in mind, however, that pushing the caffeine envelope is dangerous and can end in a major downer. If you find yourself working late evenings with less than two to three hours of sleep each night, ease back on that last cup. If you are becoming too paranoid or your stress levels become unbearable, consider reducing your intake for a couple of days and see if it helps. If, after these two days, you are still as paranoid as you normally are, then your fears must be real. Go back to your normal levels and look behind you at all times.

The effects of caffeine decrease over repeated usage. Where as a single cup of coffee might have carried you when you were in high school, you may now need three or four cups just to open your eyes. The only solution is a fate worse than a low-fat diet: Giving caffeine up altogether (see Living the Decaf Life, page 67). You'll find that you get back to your pubescent levels once you get back into the habit again.

The table on the previous page shows the different caffeine levels. Although the number of cups of coffee are specified, these parameters are by no means definitive. In fact, some hackers have experienced Mach 3 after as little as one-half cup of coffee, so the symptoms rather than the amount of coffee define the state.

Crashing

The down side of these frenzies is, of course, crashing—that lethargic, grouchy state. While experiencing the world caffeinated may help you to do it all, coming down is the price you pay. You end up incapable of doing anything, let alone coping with minor problems.

Crash Remedies

Here are some remedies to help you get through a crash.

■ *More caffeine*. Yes, this is the obvious solution and the remedy practiced more often than not. The problem, of course, is using this treatment before bedtime. The whole world feels rotten,

Falling to Earth	
STATE	**DESCRIPTION**
Losing elevation	Buzz starts to wear off; grouchiness begins to set in; you're getting impatient with people, frustrated, moody.
Tumbling	You alternate between feeling OK and losing your buzz. You try to pick up the pace, with only small results.
Crashing	You are completely void of energy, irritable, lethargic. Your motivation to do anything disappears. You develop a sudden insatiable appetite.
Catatonic	You are inanimate. All thought stops. Breathing and the basic bodily functions are all you feel capable of performing—and these cannot be done simultaneously.

and you climb into bed wanting to die. Although drinking a cup before you go to sleep may appease that feeling, doing so will doom you to working out formulas in your head all night long.

■ *Meditation*. Meditation seems to help, but most hackers want to get through these meditation sessions in under three minutes, so it is unlikely that they will find meditation to be anything but a frustrating experience. If you can slow down enough to sit still, then your meditation might work.

The key with meditation is envisioning nothingness. On caffeine, you naturally envision every teeming detail of the world. Turning this around is hard at first, but with a little practice, you will learn to turn your crashing into an uplifting experience.

- *Sports*. Hard physical labor or sports is another way of working off the grouchiness. Spending a lunch hour at the racquetball court or running is great therapy: You can slam balls instead of your boss or a whiny customer. Free solo mountain climbing has become a recent favorite of Rocky Mountain hackers. New world records have been attained by combining caffeine with the paranoia of plowing up the ground below.[1]

- Hacker cuisine. Aha!

A big vat of Cool Whip Compote (page 81) will give you a sugar high, bring your triglycerides back to normal, put a rosy spin on things, and allow you to focus on important matters at hand. Hackers instinctively seek out the best solution—mountains of sweet or starchy food to jam the caffeine circuits and gently ease the psyche into an exhausted state.

---

[1] Stay away from skydiving on caffeine: Everything goes by much too quickly. Not only will you fail to enjoy the fall, but popping the chute when you can read license plates is a serious drawback of frenzied falling.

Set and Setting— Caffeine Psychosis

Andrew Weil offered the first groundbreaking look at social drugs, of which caffeine happens to be one of the most prevalent. Weil's conclusion,[2] which is misapplied here for brevity's sake, is that individual caffeine users will introduce their own "sets" of expectations and problems into their environment. A group of users, all broadcasting their sets, and the general atmosphere of the room, form the "setting." When taken together, the set and setting will determine how enjoyable—or how frantic—the caffeine high will be. Put another way: The caffeine has no psychoactive properties itself, it merely speeds up the heart and the universe along with it. It is this magnification of our collective mental states that adds that certain over-the-top quality to our caffeinated rides.

It is unrealistic to suggest that five cups of coffee will help you sustain peak sailing when you are going through a messy divorce. The only thing that caffeine will do to you at that point is make you want to invest in an assault rifle. Your caffeine ride is influenced almost entirely by the events of your day, your emotional well-being, and the well-being of those around you. Some

---

[2] Andrew Weil, The Natural Mind. (Boston: Houghton-Mifflin, 1986): 21-30.

additional words of advice concerning bad trips (yes, we thought they were only limited to psychedelics, but any drug causes them, and caffeine more than most):

■ If you are under a great deal of stress and the caffeine is pushing you into paranoia, quit coffee for a number of days. Wait until you are out of your gloom before drinking coffee again.

■ If those around you are going through tough times, get on their case. They may erupt, but it is the best way to help them let go. When they do, politely excuse yourself so that you do not get hurt. No need to stick around for friendship's sake—these people need professional help.

In the end, you may find yourself scavenging around in the muck of your life or mentally playing out gloomy scenarios (losing your job, getting a job, or whatever). In these cases, recognize that the caffeine may be messing you up. Just stop the coffee! Your days will brighten up, and your friends will return.

Living the Decaf Life

Some hackers have sworn off the drug completely.

You do not absolutely need caffeine to hack, but you will need a substitute. You can produce mountains of work without the stuff by hooking into the "adrenaline of life," as a friend once said. Connect to any abiding paranoia or fear, expand it out of all proportion until you think you are going to die of it, and then begin hacking as if your life and sanity depended on it. There is no better state of natural frenzy.

Many of the drinks described in this next section are heavily caffeinated. Most have evolved from a hacker's continual push to infuse more caffeine per gulp than is normally served at your better restaurants.

Hammerheads (Coffee Drinks)

There is no finer way to hit Mach 1 or any frenzied state of your choice than with classic coffee concoctions—combinations of one or more coffee drinks with powdered chocolate and a squirt of cream. These drinks are blended for taste, fortified for optimum caffeine jolts, and drunk one or two at a time with care.

2 cups	**coffee (brewed or instant)**
2 demi cups	**espresso (brewed or powdered)**
2 tsp.	**powdered coffee**
2 tsp.	**powdered chocolate or chocolate syrup**
splash	**cream**
dash	**sugar**
1 second	**whipped cream**

1. Brew your regular coffee, or mix it from instant.
2. Mix in the espresso and other ingredients, topping with whipped cream.
3. Serve hot and frothy in a large cup or bowl.

SERVES: 1 OR 2

Hot Fudge Smoothies

 This wonderful combination of bananas, hot fudge, and ice cream is perfect for those late hacking sessions when you have the munchies but cannot pull yourself away from your machine.

1 large bottle	**hot fudge sauce**
2	**overripe bananas**
1 pint	**ice cream (vanilla, chocolate, or coffee flavor)**

Floppy Doilies

A practical use for corrupted floppies is as doilies for drinks. Available in a range of colors, floppies can be stacked in their original cartons and brought out to protect your coffee table when you are serving drinks there, or use them alongside your computer to protect your printouts. (See "Emergency Utensils," page 14.)

3 tbsp.	**milk**
splash	**cream**
dash	**sugar**

1. If you have a blender, put all the ingredients in it and blend until thick. Otherwise, turn the ingredients into a large bowl and mash with a fork, large spoon, or potato masher until lumpy.
2. Pour into a large glass and serve frosty.

SERVES: 1

Coke Floats

 The classic float is unbeatable for late night dinners, a snack, or a dessert. Keep the Coke cold for best results and serve in a large bowl.

64 ounces Coke	
1 pint	**ice cream (vanilla, chocolate, or coffee flavor)**
squirt	**whipped cream**

1. Pour the Coke into a large bowl and heap the ice cream gently on top. If the mixture starts to foam, bend down and slurp off the excess. If you are serving this treat at a dinner party, do the foam slurp in a secluded room.
2. Serve immediately with whipped cream and drink or eat communally from the bowl. Serve extra long straws and spoons to prevent concussions.

SERVES: 1 OR 2

Melted Ice Cream Malaise

This recipe was first discovered after a large dinner party turned into a snore-a-thon, with everybody—including the host—asleep in the living room. A large tub of ice cream had been left out and melted. When the group awoke and got ready for class, the melted ice cream was the perfect breakfast drink. Rocky road and peppermint swirl make some of the best concoctions.

1 gallon   ice cream

1. Leave the ice cream out for about 4 hours until completely melted.
2. Decant and serve cold.

SERVES: 1 OR 2

Jolt Bolt

For a friendly picker-upper in the morning, this drink mixes the zesty taste of cinnamon with the frenzy that only Jolt cola can deliver.

1 can   Jolt cola
2   cinnamon candy sticks

1. Pour the cola into a tall glass and add the candy sticks. Stir until candy is completely dissolved.
2. Add ice and serve.

SERVES: 1

Beet Juice Cocktail

Beets have long been a favorite hacker food. Apart from their nutritional value, beets have a unique ability to dye a hacker's insides red. This can be a source of endless fun for the hacker set. Beet juice should be collected and served as a cocktail.

1 quart   beet juice
1/2 cup   coffee
dash   soy sauce

1. Mix the ingredients together.
2. Add ice and serve.

SERVES: 1 OR 2

Earthshakes

There are no thicker shakes made. The only problem with these shakes is their tendency to get lodged in your throat if inhaled too quickly. Always warn novices not to exceed the speed limit for shakes—about one mouthful every 10 seconds.

1 quart   ice cream (any flavor)
3 tbsp.   milk
splash   cream
dash   sugar

1. Use a blender if you have it to turn the ice cream into a shake consistency. Otherwise, let the ice cream soften for 5 minutes and mash with a fork

69

(if the ice cream has nuts or frozen pieces of fruit, warn your guests).

2. Mix well with other ingredients.

3. Pour into a large glass and serve frosty.

SERVES: 1 OR 2

Whipped Jell-O Drinks

 Originally, Jell-O drinks started with leftover Jell-O in the refrigerator and a thirsty group of hackers. Nowadays, these drinks are served cold with a little liquor. For real fun, play around with the flavors and types of liquor.

1 pint	prepared Jell-O (green or red)
2 cups	Kool-Aid, prepared
1 tbsp.	brown sugar
1 cup	rum
dash	nutmeg
1 second	whipped cream (for garnish)

1. Combine all of the ingredients except the whipped cream in a pitcher and mix vigorously with a fork. If you have a blender, blend ingredients at low for 30 seconds. The liquid should remain lumpy. If you use red Jell-O, then use green Kool-Aid; if green Jell-O, red Kool-Aid; and so on.

2. Serve over ice. Finish with a dollop of whipped cream.

SERVES: 2 OR 3

Variations:

Jell-O Juleps. Use lime Kool-Aid with strawberry Jell-O. Mix with mint liqueur.

Jell-O Margaritas. Mix tequila, triple sec, lime Jell-O, and lemon Kool-Aid. Serve in salted glasses.

Irish Jell-O. Blend whiskey, coffee, and red Jell-O. Finish with whipped cream.

Chili Beer

 Growing in popularity, chili beer combines the great taste of a cold beer with red hot chili for extra pizzazz.

32 ounces	beer (in bottle)
1 can	whole green chilies
1	lime, sliced, or 2 tbsp. lime juice
dash	cayenne

1. One hour before serving, open the beer and pour a couple of ounces of it into a glass. Stuff the chilies into the beer bottle using a straw or thin stick (do not try this with your fingers or you may get stuck). Replace cap.

2. Keep beer in the refrigerator until ready to serve.

3. Before serving, place a lime slice or splash of lime juice and a dash of cayenne in the bottom of each glass. Pour beer into glasses.

SERVES: 2 OR 3

Variation:

Chili Cheese Beer. Add a dollop of Cheez Whiz to each glass and watch the froth when you pour in the beer. Serve cold.

Hacker Laced Ice Tea

 A sure late evening cure to a frazzled day, this drink incorporates almost every bottle in the liquor cabinet to create an alcoholic punch that soothes the savage hacker.

1 pint	**dark rum**
1 pint	**vodka**
1 pint	**whisky**
1 pint	**tequila**
1 jigger	**triple sec**
1	**lime, sliced**

1. Mix the liquor into a large pitcher over ice.
2. Serve in glasses with a lime slice.

   SERVES: 2 OR 3

Brandy Buckets

 Normally served in sedate snifters, brandy is meant to be enjoyed. Serving it hacker-style is a great way to spread the merriment and enjoy more brandy in one sitting than Alistair Cooke has seen in a lifetime.

1 gallon   brandy

1. Decant the brandy into a large bowl and serve with a ladle.

   SERVES: 2

Hacker Margaritas

 Fresh margaritas are a pain to make. The mixes these days are a great approximation. By doubling the alcohol content of the drink, you can disguise the powdery taste and increase the overall volume of conversation.

3 packages	**margarita mix**
3 quarts	**tequila**
1	**lime, sliced**

1. Stir the margarita mix with the tequila until the powder disappears from the bottom of the pitcher.
2. Place the lime slices on top and serve over ice.

   SERVES: 2 OR 3

Variation:

Hacker Strawberry Margarita. Add a package of frozen strawberries and stir well. Although the strawberries sink to the bottom, the novelty of fruit in a glass will make this drink a lasting favorite.

Recommended Samurai Movies

Hacker cuisine can be enjoyed with almost any distraction; however, Japanese samurai movies offer some of the best material for late evening get-togethers. Some of the recommended movies are the following:

- *Genroku Chushingura* (The Loyal Forty-Seven Ronin) Parts I and II. Directed by Kenji Mizoguchi. (1942) This classic story follows the forty-seven vassals of Lord Asano who vow their loyalty after their lord was ordered to commit ritual suicide (seppuku) at the hands of the unscrupulous Lord Kira. Forced to disperse and to serve no master (thus becoming ronin), they plot to take their revenge exactly one year later. Kira is hunted down, and the forty-seven ronin avenge their lord's murder.

- *Miyamoto Musashi; Ichijoji no ketto; Ketto Ganyujima* (The Samurai Trilogy). Directed by Hiroshi Inagaki. (1954–1955) These three films follow the legendary Miyamoto Musashi (a part played for all its bawdiness by Toshiro Mifune). Musashi single-handedly slays countless enemies but only later in life discovers the true source of his powers. In a climactic ending, Musashi takes on his archrival Sasaki Kojiro (played by Koji Tsurata). Equipped with only a wooden sword that he fashions on the way to Ganryu Island, Musashi recognizes that Kojiro will die even before the fight begins, for Kojiro has absentmindedly disposed of his scabbard.

- *Shichinin no samurai* (Seven Samurai). Directed by Akira Kurosawa. (1954) Starring Toshiro Mifune. This timeless film follows seven ronin as they set out to protect a village from a group of marauding bandits. At the time, the film was the largest production undertaken in Japan, costing about $500,000 and taking over a year to film.

- *Kakushi torideno sanakunin* (The Hidden Fortress) Directed by Akira Kurosawa. (1958) Starring Toshiro Mifune. Two farmers meet up with a mysterious warrior (Mifune) on their return from a battle. The warrior, who is actually a famous general, convinces them to accompany him on his travels to uncover hidden treasures. With him is the princess from the defeated clan, traveling in disguise. The tale is one of greed and loyalty and is rumored to be the inspiration for George Lucas's *Star Wars*.

Desserts

DESSERTS HAVE TRADITIONALLY been served throughout a hacker meal. It is not unusual to find Foo Bars (page 75) served alongside a hearty Breadball Marinara (page 45), cinnamon buns have been used as dinner rolls for many years, and sundaes of various flavors have replaced the traditional turkey at Thanksgiving get-togethers. Whereas sorbets have been used to cleanse the palate at fancy meals, hackers use desserts to completely inundate the senses throughout dinner. It is the Roman orgy approach to pacing a meal, and it comes from the basic view of a dinner as the coup de grâce to the day. There should be as much overload as possible, so there is no question when the meal is over.

Of course, most hackers sleep after they eat, but with a couple of Hammerheads (page 67), the evening can continue into the early hours.

The desserts in this section fall into three main categories:

1. *Chocolate overload.* These dishes are built on the knowledge that there can never be too much chocolate in a dessert. The recipes combine many varieties of chocolate and aim at satiating the most ardent chocoholic's cravings—at least for one meal.

2. *Sugar nirvana.* Not every hacker craves sugar highs, but most come off their all-night hacking in a caffeinated frenzy. Blood sugar tends to be quite low and a burst of sugar goes a long way to cushioning the inevitable crash (see page 65). Recipes in this category are usually high in the three basic sugar food groups: brown sugar, refined sugar, and syrupy sugar. Little or no fructose is used, since it is a diluted sugar that lacks the real punch of these other varieties.

3. *Cakey creations.* Finally, there are the cakey desserts, usually filled with Twinkies or other confectionery. These recipes do not overload the taste buds with any specific taste (like

chocolate); rather, they aim at filling the last vestiges of hacker hunger. Even after a rather large meal of Spam Oinkers (page 52) or Hot Dog Stroganoff (page 50), a hacker may have a little room left for dessert. Cakey desserts fill these spaces like mortar on a cracked wall.

It goes without saying that eating desserts is a messy affair. Whether it is Loose Pudding Surprise (below) or Jell-O Fingers in Peanut Sauce (page 77), there is no graceful way to eat the following recipes. These desserts are meant to be eaten fast and furiously.

Guarding Your Keyboard

One of the most unfortunate places to drip is the keyboard. Most hackers will lean to one side when eating, but this is not always possible. Bringing out the plastic keyboard cover is not always convenient. (Many a hacker has complained that doing so stifles his creativity). So one reader, Bertrand Lloyd of Milwaukee, Wisconsin, suggests placing the dipping bowl directly in front of the keyboard. As he explains, "The path from dip to mouth never crosses the keyboard's air space. Think of the keyboard as France and your mouth as Libya. Now, if you were President Reagan, how would you attack? My answer, move France to somewhere closer to Siberia and out of the main flight trajectory."

Loose Pudding Surprise

This hacker classic uses chocolate milk and chocolate pudding stirred to a lumpy consistency. It can be mixed with nuts or pieces of cookies. Traditionally, this crowd pleaser was served at puppy weanings in a folded newspaper. Nowadays, standard bowls are more common. This dessert is a refreshing treat for all ages.

1 cup	**mashed raisins**
1 quart	**chocolate pudding**
dash	**nutmeg**
1 pint	**chocolate milk**

1. Mash the raisins and mix well into the pudding. Add the nutmeg.
2. In a bowl, add the chocolate milk slowly until the mixture appears lumpy and uneven. Do not stir too much.
3. Serve warm or cold, with spoons or straws.

   SERVES: 2 OR 3

Cold PopTart Soup

Cold soups have long been a tradition in sophisticated European cooking. This classic makes use of soft drinks and PopTarts for a unique flavor. Serve as a dessert or fancy late evening snack after drinks. It is sure to be an eye-opener.

4	PopTarts
2 cups	cold soda
1 tsp.	sugar
dash	nutmeg
dash	cinnamon

1. Crumble the PopTarts into a bowl. They should be roughly 2-inch irregular shapes.
2. Add the remaining ingredients and stir gently.
3. Set aside in the refrigerator for about 2 minutes, until the PopTarts are slightly soggy.
4. Serve cold.

SERVES: 2 OR 3

Jell-O Squares in Tangy Mayonnaise

Jell-O now comes ready to eat in the deli case. Although some die-hards will want to make it from scratch, you needn't bother. This old-time favorite updates the basic recipe with innovative sauces. Wedge the squares in a bowl of the mayonnaise mixture or place into a mold. Be careful—the mixtures tend to be runny.

2 pints	prepared Jell-O (green or red)
1 cup	mayonnaise
2 tbsp.	brown sugar
splash	milk
1/4 tsp.	chili pepper
dash	cinnamon
dash	nutmeg
dash	cloves

1. Turn the Jell-O onto your counter and cut into 1-inch squares. Put into a bowl.
2. In a separate bowl, stir the remaining ingredients until the mixture has the consistency of pudding. Drop the Jell-O squares into the mixture. The higher the drop, the deeper the square will submerge. Save this last step for serving to add some panache to your dessert.

SERVES: 2 OR 3

Variation:

Jell-O Squares in Hot Fudge. Substitute a small jar of hot fudge for the mayonnaise. Zap the mixture for 1 minute and serve hot.

Foo Bars

This classic hacker dish (also referred to as Fubar) is named after foo programs, which are used regularly by hackers as counterexamples to well-known theorems. The bars make a great accompaniment to Jell-O squares or ice cream.

1 large jar	hot fudge sauce
1 cup	crushed Butterfingers
2	crushed graham crackers
2 tbsp.	brown sugar
dash	cinnamon
12 large	chocolate chip cookies

1. Zap the jar of hot fudge until it is warm. (Do not forget to remove the lid.)
2. In a large bowl, combine the hot fudge, crushed candy, crackers, and spices. Stir until well mixed and thick. Add more graham crackers until the mixture is stiff.
3. Scoop the mixture between two cookies so that it forms a sandwich. Serve immediately. (Be warned: This is a messy one!)

SERVES: 2 OR 3

Twinkie Casserole

There is nothing like a large casserole for dessert, especially after a main course that did not quite go over with your crowd. Keep the ingredients for this dessert on hand for such an emergency. Presentation is everything with this dish. Each scrumptious layer will be a surprise for your guests.

2 dozen	Twinkies
1 large jar	caramel topping
1 bag	miniature marshmallows

1 large jar	hot fudge
1 tsp.	cinnamon
dash	brown sugar
2 dozen	Oreos

1. Line the bottom of a casserole dish or a large plate with the Twinkies.
2. Pour the caramel topping evenly over the Twinkies and smooth with a knife.
3. Pour the miniature marshmallows over the top of the caramel until it is completely hidden.
4. Pour the hot fudge over the marshmallows.
5. Sprinkle the spices over the hot fudge.
6. Layer the Oreos on top of the casserole.
7. Serve immediately.

SERVES: 2 OR 3

Variation:

Twinkie and Ice Cream Casserole. Before putting the Oreos on top, add a thick layer of vanilla or coffee ice cream on top. A great summer blowout!

Chopped Candy Bar Ice Cream

Some of the Heath Bar ice creams got their start in hacker halls around the country. Chopped Candy Bar Ice Cream uses a 50:50 mixture of candy bars and vanilla or chocolate ice cream for a wonderfully rich dessert. Add hot fudge and turn this classic into a great sundae.

2 pounds	**candy bars**
1 gallon	**ice cream (vanilla or chocolate)**
1 pint	**hot fudge sauce (optional)**

1. Chop the candy bars into 1-inch pieces and freeze until ready to serve.
2. Empty the ice cream into a large bowl and top with the chopped candy bars. Add hot fudge if you like.
3. Serve cold with spoons.

SERVES: 2 OR 3

Variations:

Pothole Ice Cream. Add miniature marshmallows to the mixture, and you've got a combination that puts rocky road to shame.

Baby Ruth Ice Cream Dip. Instead of eating the ice cream with spoons, use frozen Baby Ruths or Snickers bars to dip.

Cookie Ice Cream Mush. Grind Oreos and other of your favorites into a fine powder and stir in softened ice cream.

Jell-O Fingers in Peanut Sauce

Jell-O makes the perfect finger food. This easy-to-eat snack is great fun for a party. Ladle the sauce over your squares or serve them on the side for dunking.

2 pints	**prepared Jell-O (green or red)**
1 cup	**peanut butter**
1/2 cup	**chocolate sauce**
1 tbsp.	**brown sugar**
splash	**milk**
dash	**cinnamon**
dash	**white pepper (for zest)**
dash	**nutmeg**

1. Turn the Jell-O onto the counter and cut into 1-inch strips. Put into a bowl.
2. In a separate bowl, mix the remaining ingredients until the consistency of white glue. For dunking, keep this mixture in the bowl; otherwise, ladle it over the Jell-O strips and serve immediately.
3. To eat, lift a Jell-O strip by one end and lower it carefully into the sauce. The strip should emerge slightly gooey.

SERVES: 2 OR 3

Variation:

Jell-O Fingers with Mashed Banana Sauce. Substitute 1 cup of mashed bananas for the peanut butter. Stir loosely and serve cold.

Jell-O Crepes

This French classic is recreated with a more modern filling. Frozen crepes may be purchased at most

grocery stores, but if you cannot find them, use flour tortillas rolled in a little sugar. Toothpicks hold the rolls in place.

1 pint	**prepared Jell-O (green or red)**
1 dozen	**frozen crepes, or flour tortillas with sugar**
1 tbsp.	**brown sugar**
dash	**cinnamon**
dash	**nutmeg**

1. Cut the Jell-O into 1-inch strips and lay them out on the counter.

2. If you are using tortillas, coat each tortilla in sugar (you may need to moisten the tortillas first). Place 1 or 2 Jell-O strips on a crepe. Sprinkle the sugar, cinnamon, and nutmeg on top, then form into an enchilada shape. Fasten with a toothpick.

3. Stack on a serving dish and zap for one minute in a microwave. Make sure that the Jell-O does not break up.

SERVES: 2 OR 3

Variations:

Jell-O Crepes with Hot Fudge. Smear 1 teaspoon of hot fudge on each crepe before folding.

Jell-O Enchiladas in Chocolate Sauce. Lay the finished crepes in a square cooking pan. Pour 1 cup of chocolate sauce over them. To serve, use a pie cutter. This recipe works great if you accidentally zapped the crepes too long in the microwave and the Jell-O turns slightly watery.

78

Mashed Banana Cups

This fun dessert uses leftover bananas and the small graham cracker cups that can be purchased in most grocery stores.

6	**old bananas**
6 to 8	**graham cracker crusts (small kind)**
1 tbsp.	**brown sugar**
1 tbsp.	**mayonnaise**
dash	**nutmeg**
1 second	**whipped cream (for garnish)**

1. Combine the bananas, brown sugar, mayonnaise, and nutmeg in a bowl and mash with a fork until smooth.

2. Scoop mixture into the graham cracker crusts. Finish with a dollop of whipped cream.

SERVES: 4 OR 5

Minced Jell-O Pie

For Jell-O that has dried up in your refrigerator, this dish is a sweet substitute for mincemeat pie which never tasted that good to begin with. Use pre-baked pie shells and canned frosting to hold the Jell-O together. Serve chilled with whipped cream on top. No one will ever know that this started out as leftover Jell-O.

6 to 8 cups	leftover Jell-O
1 can	vanilla frosting
1 can	chopped nuts
1	baked pie shell
1 cup	whipped cream
dash	nutmeg

1. Turn the Jell-O onto a clean counter. Chop into tiny bits with a sharp knife. (Alternately, you may use a fork to get the Jell-O into a granular size.)
2. Combine the Jell-O, frosting, nutmeg, and nuts in a large bowl. Stir until thoroughly mixed.
3. Pile mixture up in the pie shell and coat the top with whipped cream before serving. Serve this pie cold.

SERVES: 2 OR 3

Chopped Candy Bar Cake

Tired of those old store-bought chocolate cakes? This recipe is a quick cure. Using cold candy bars and a sharp knife, minor surgery is performed on your favorite dessert, turning a tasty cake into a decadent mutation. Keep fingers well out of the way when operating.

2 pounds	candy bars
1 large	ready-to-eat cake (chocolate is my favorite)
1 can	frosting
1 can	chopped nuts
10 seconds	whipped cream

1. Chop the candy bars into 1-inch chunks with a sharp knife.
2. Remove the cake from its box and place it on a clean counter. Using a sharp knife, cut the cake horizontally so there are a top half and a bottom half. (If you already cut the cake vertically because you thought you knew this recipe, you might as well turn your dessert into Cake and Ice Cream Sandwiches—see next recipe.)
3. Carefully set the top half of the cake aside. Do not place the top half on its frosting side. Press the candy bars into the lower half of the cake, keeping them equally spaced. Set any leftover pieces aside.
4. Place a layer of frosting over the top of the candy pieces until level, then replace the top half of the cake. The cake should not look tilted. If it does, add frosting on top of the lower side.
5. Sprinkle nuts and leftover chunks of candy on top, then squirt on the whipped cream.

SERVES: 2 OR 3

Cake and Ice Cream Sandwiches

This is the jumbo version of ice cream sandwiches made from store-bought cakes and softened ice cream. Think of your cake as a loaf of bread, your box of ice cream as unsliced bologna, and your can of frosting as mustard. From this viewpoint, sandwiches are a logical extension.

1 large	**ready-to-eat cake (chocolate is my favorite)**
1 can	**frosting**
1 box	**long toothpicks (optional)**
1 quart	**ice cream**

1. Remove the cake from its box and place it on a clean counter. Using a sharp knife, cut the cake into slices like bread.
2. On the counter next to the cake, turn out the box of ice cream and cut into 1-inch slices.
3. Place a square of ice cream between two pieces of cake with a smear of frosting. Fasten with a toothpick.
4. Keep in the freezer until ready to serve.

SERVES: 2 OR 3

Butterfinger Casserole

This dish is often mistaken for a main course but was originally served warm with ice cream for a powerful engine-revver for late night hacking. It is best to buy the Butterfingers in bulk, since they are always in demand around a hacker apartment.

2 dozen	**Butterfinger candy bars**
1 large jar	**chocolate syrup**
1/2 bag	**miniature marshmallows**
1 cup	**jelly beans**
2 cans	**whipped cream**
1 tsp.	**cinnamon**
2 tsp.	**brown sugar**

1. In a large bowl, break the Butterfingers and mix with the syrup, marshmallows, and jelly beans until the mixture is lumpy.
2. Zap until warm.
3. Pile on whipped cream and sprinkle with cinnamon and brown sugar before serving.

SERVES: 2 OR 3

The Leaning Tower

There is nothing more exciting than two dozen donuts teetering on the edge of a table. Their only salvation is your stomach. This classic dish, inspired by the famous Italian monument to gravity, uses donuts as the bricks and frosting as the cement. It is best to construct this tower in the location where you plan to serve it.

2 dozen	**donuts**
1 can	**frosting**

1. On a large plate, carefully place one donut on top of another with a little extra frosting as mortar. Use the cake donuts on the bottom and the fluffier ones on top to prevent total disaster.
2. Stack the donuts until they form a single vertical column.
3. Serve with coffee.

SERVES: 2 OR 3

Chocolate Huff and Puff

 This favorite hacker fare uses chocolate milk mix to compress chocolate pudding into a thick, rich mixture. It is a favorite of graphics hackers, who regularly "huff and puff" images for transmission. (The name denotes the compressing and decompressing of data.)

1 quart chocolate pudding
1 1/2 cups chocolate milk mix
1 tbsp. cocoa (optional)

1. In a large bowl, combine the ingredients and stir until the mixture is very thick and chocolatey.
2. Serve as a dip or with a spoon.

SERVES: 2 OR 3

Cool Whip Compote

 Although the name suggests fruit, this dish is usually made with candy bars. For best results, keep the candy bars cool before serving.

1 pound Milk Duds
1 large tub Cool Whip
1 cup chocolate syrup

1. Chop the candy bars into 1-inch squares and stir into the Cool Whip. Make sure that none of the candy bars show on the surface.
2. Prior to serving, ladle on the syrup.
3. Serve with coffee.

SERVES: 2 OR 3

Dipped Fruit

 You should never have to serve fruit for dessert. There is nothing more disappointing to a guest than wading through a main course and finding out that only fruit is being served for dessert. Hackers would probably walk out at this point in the meal. However, as a compromise, dipped fruit offers a little variety to a bad dessert idea.

1 quart chocolate syrup
1 pound fruit

1. Prior to serving, dip the fruit in the syrup. Arrange on a plate and serve. (Keep in mind that bananas and grapefruit should be peeled first. Watermelons simply do not work in this recipe.) Napkins are required for this dish, which can get a little messy.

SERVES: 2 OR 3

Leftover Macaroni and Ice Cream Pie

This bulkier dessert combines the practicality of getting rid of old food with the coolness of ice cream. Your guests will love it, but make sure that you serve enough wine during dinner.

2 cups	leftover macaroni
1 gallon	ice cream
1 cup	chocolate syrup
1 cup	chopped nuts
1	baked pie shell
10 seconds	whipped cream (canned)

1. Mix the macaroni and ice cream until smooth. Add the syrup and nuts and quickly toss.
2. Ladle mixture into the pie shell and put back into freezer. Prior to serving, add the whipped cream.

SERVES: 2 OR 3

Three-Pigs PopTarts

This is a variation of beggar's chicken, the Chinese dish that was discovered when a house burned down on a cooking chicken. Under the rubble, the chicken had been cooked slowly in a pile of spices and tasted great. Three-Pigs PopTarts uses the fallen house analogy from the fairy tale. In this case, the house is made of PopTarts. As the saying goes, "Those in PopTart houses should not throw toasters." This dish is a great conversation piece.

1 can	chocolate frosting
6 to 8	PopTarts
1 quart	vanilla ice cream
1 jar	hot fudge sauce, cold
6 seconds	whipped cream
dash	nutmeg
dash	brown sugar
1	wine bottle

1. Form a box out of PopTarts on a flat plate. Use chocolate frosting to hold the sides together.
2. Working quickly, fill the bottom half of the box with vanilla ice cream.
3. Layer cold hot fudge sauce about 1/2″ thick. Add a second layer of ice cream and another layer of hot fudge.
4. Squirt whipping cream on top and sprinkle with nutmeg and brown sugar.
5. Complete the PopTart house, sealing and decorating it with the chocolate frosting.
6. Store in freezer until ready. Upon serving, hand the wine bottle to the wolf of choice to break the house with a swift clobber on the roof. Scoop up the wreckage with the broken PopTarts.

SERVES: 2 OR 3

Appendixes

A. The Zen of Cleaning Up

CLEANLINESS IS NOT high on a hacker's priority list. It usually ranks just below having the right length of shoe laces—important but not paramount. However, the act of cleaning up can be awfully time consuming, and a hacker hates to waste time. To this end this appendix provides some guidelines to cleaning up that can save valuable time while leaving your cooking area relatively clean.

Before You Begin

The best time to minimize cleanup is before you start. You can stop right there and face absolutely no cleanup. However, most of us are so hungry when we first set foot into the kitchen that we fail to consider the consequences of opening cans right and left. Opening up a large bag of chips or setting out some leftovers for noshing will allow you to think more clearly. In most cases, you will want to choose a menu, arrange the necessary ingredients and implements on the counter, and begin your preparation.

Some words of advice here:

- Cut your ingredients directly into the actual cooking pot or pan.
- When emptying cans, place your bowl or pan directly underneath the can opener. This way you can catch any spills while greatly shortening the path to the bowl.
- Always use the fewest possible dishes in the preparation of any meal. To eliminate the bowl, mix ingredients in the pan.
- Always serve food from the pan. Better yet, eat from the pan! Not only will you get the meal hot, but you will also eliminate serving bowls and utensils.
- Pour all soups and liquid meals directly from the pot or pan into your bowl sans ladle. You will probably miss often until you get the hang of this motion, but that's what a mop is for.[1]

---

[1] Don't feel you have to mop immediately. Sit down and enjoy your meal first. Then remember the floor.

- Move all food from the main cooking pan to your plate with your own eating fork.
- Use paper plates and cups. To clean up, take your plates from the table or couch where you left them, scrape, and add to the recycle bag. (Or rinse and store for another use.)
- Do not use a knife or spoon with dinner. These just need to be cleaned up.
- Dunk wherever possible. Not only is this style of eating enjoyable, but also you do not have to use utensils—just your fingers. A quick lick after dinner and they're clean!

The solution to cleanup is discipline—a very ugly word, especially around food, where the laws of nature conspire—so let's just forget discipline here. Instead, simply eliminate any excess kitchen equipment. Reduce your arsenal of cooking utensils to the absolute minimum (see the chapter Batterie de Cuisine). Throw out old pots and pans (the Salvation Army or thrift stores would love these, by the way): keep only one. Have one serving spoon for a special occasion and get rid of the rest. Keep your glasses to the absolute minimum. A couple of complete settings of silverware is enough. One large dip bowl will suffice.

In this way, you will naturally reduce cleanup time because you no longer own enough dishes to make the process time consuming. With recyclable, disposable plates, cups, and bowls, you will enjoy a maintenance-free collection of eating gear.

Eating for the Optimal 'Clean'

Most of us think that cleanup should come to mind after a meal is completed, but you can begin the cleanup process even before you finish your meal. Our personal eating techniques have been handed down for the most part these days by Emily Post. We are much too mannered for our own good, and certainly our enjoyment of food suffers.

Eat to enjoy, but also eat efficiently. Here are some more rules of thumb that can make a big difference when it comes time for cleanup:

- Finish what is on your plate, no matter how much there is. Yes, at the risk of sounding like your mother, there are starving people everywhere today—not just in China. Look around you! Look at the homeless and the hungry sprawled on the evening news. People *are* hungry. You *should* feel guilty throwing food away. So clean your plate! Encourage your guests to finish their meals as well.

  With all the food gone, you will reduce scraping time by 50 percent.
- Lick your utensils, plates, and—where necessary—guests. This will bring you closer to the ideal "clean."

  The French recommend running a piece of bread around the perimeter of the plate. This excellent method can replace the tongue-to-plate accidents that are common these days.

■ If one of your recipes fails and there is a lot left to finish, move the plate to the floor for your dog. (If you don't have a dog, you might consider one at this point — they make great pets and can be invaluable for cleanup.)

The goal is clean plates and utensils at the end of the meal—at least they should look very clean. Take paper plates and cups to the recycling bin, and you are done.

Cleaning Your Screen

It is inevitable that some day you will be eating quietly while listening to a favorite radio station. You hear a joke, and the next thing you know, your computer screen is sprayed with dip.

The natural inclination is to use a shirt sleeve, but a soft cloth with a light soaking of rubbing alcohol works wonders. First wipe off the excess food, then, with a clean portion of the cloth, wipe the screen until the images are once again clear.

Ratproofing

All cleanup should be saved for the next day, preferably in the morning. This allows you to eat and sleep or eat and work without the fear of interrupting either activity with cleaning. There's nothing worse than wading through a pile of cleanup after a great dinner.

You will need to protect your dirty dishes from cockroaches, flies, rats, ants, and other scavengers. Many come unseen at night. Most of us like to think that these varmints make homes in other neighborhoods, when in reality every imaginable scavenger inhabits our own apartments or homes. Although you may be lucky to escape them today, you are an easy target tomorrow if you leave loads of food sitting on your dining table or stuck between the pillows of your couch.

The most important step in any cleanup is preserving dirty dishes until you are forced to clean them. The technique is relatively easy, as follows:

■ Before getting up from your meal, scrape all leftovers onto one plate. Determine whether you are going to eat this new creation, remembering that many a new recipe was invented at this juncture.

■ With a napkin, wipe all crumbs and spills off your chest before attempting to stand. Place the dish to the side of your chest and blow any crumbs onto it. Not only will this clean your eating surface, but also you can test your bearing after a number of beers.

85

■ If you are going to eat the rest, store the leftovers in the refrigerator leftovers bin (see Leftover Strategies, page 87). Otherwise, scrape the contents of the single plate into the garbage.

■ Pile everything into the sink except your paper utensils, which can go directly into the recycling bin.

■ To keep the creatures away, stopper your sink and fill it to cover any dishes and pots with water or, alternately, put the dirty dishes in your freezer. If the dishes are pretty dirty, put them into a plastic bag.

■ Let sit for up to one week or until you need the dishes, whichever occurs first.

The 'C' Word

Cleaning up is the biggest waste of time there is. There is never a good time for it. The only thing that you can do to make it more palatable is to do it quickly. Music or altered states do not seem to make this activity any more enjoyable. Wherever possible, suggest that your guest get a head start on the dishes while you hit the john. This seems to work the best, since you can stay in there the longest. (As a guest, you may want to make some perfunctory attempts to get started, then put your feet up. It is always acceptable to say, "I didn't know where you keep your things. . . .")

The easiest time to clean up is immediately before you need a particular dish. At this point, when you are still ravenous, you feel more motivated.

Other rules of thumb are the following:

■ Before washing, remember to thaw your dishes to prevent cracking.

■ Place a dab of dish-washing liquid on a scouring pad while you run the tap. With about six strokes, scour your pan. Rinse and dry. If any three-dimensional particles remain on the surface, they will become part of the next meal. However, if the gunk is burned on and covers more than half the pan, discard the pan.

■ For plates, three strokes should be enough. Rinse and dry.

■ For utensils, one stroke will do. Rinse and dry.

■ Don't bother putting the dishes in your cabinet. You'll just have to take them out again. Keep them on the drying rack.

Try to keep your cleanup time under five minutes. Racing against the clock will keep cleanup activities somewhat interesting.

If you have had any episodes of intestinal cramping, vomiting more than usual, or headaches, you may be rushing the cleanup too much. Also, be sure to use soap to clean. This step is important—if a mossy coating forms over your teeth, you probably are not rinsing well enough. Increase the strength of your tap and hold the dishes under it for a longer period of time.

If your guests are cutting themselves when they try to lick the plates, you may not be cleaning well enough. Dried food is also known to be a leading

cause of tongue bruises. If these are occurring with increasing frequency, it may be time to buy new plates or begin using paper plates.

Leftover Strategies

The world contains two types of people: Those who save and those who throw out. Before determining the best strategy for saving any leftovers, determine your type. Do you love to ferret away items in boxes or save papers you no longer need? If so, you are a classic pack rat and will probably want to save every leftover. If you discard items as soon as you've seen them once—such as bills, books, and girlfriends—then you are definitely not a pack rat, but research has shown that even people like you have been known to make a complete 180 degree reversal—saving food even though you normally toss out nonfood items of seemingly equivalent value.

In either case, you will find that leftovers can make excellent ingredients for another meal, or they can be eaten the next day either as an appetizer or a cold breakfast or even reheated for dinner. On average, you should be able to eat the same meal about four times in a row before tiring of it.

Here are some rules of thumb about leftovers:

■ Keep a single plastic bin in your refrigerator for your leftovers. This will save on containers, and you will be able to find the lid!

Choose the size of the leftover bin based on the volume of leftovers currently in your refrigerator. Start with a quart container if you are new to saving leftovers. One- and two-gallon containers are not uncommon for experienced hackers.

■ Determine first if you enjoyed the dish the first time around. This is the main reason to hold onto leftovers, so don't try to kid yourself.

If you decide the dish is worth keeping, ladle the new leftovers to the side of existing remains in the bin. Use colored toothpicks to identify dishes if they look similar.

■ If you fill up the first level of your leftover bin, begin a new level on top of the existing one.

Composting with Leftovers

With our planet in dire need of rejuvenation, start a composting heap in your yard (or right there in your kitchen, if you have room). Any leftover that is past its prime (say, after six months of refrigeration) can be placed into the heap. Leave the heap in a warm spot. If you are composting in your kitchen, cover the heap and keep it warm. When the compost is ripe enough, scatter over your plants.

Keep in mind that when reusing your leftovers, you'll need to start at the bottom and work up.

- After about a month, you may want to either throw the leftovers out or freeze them for doorstops.
- To reuse your leftovers, keep in mind that you have three basic choices: You can use them as ingredients for new dishes, you can serve them au natural to relive the enjoyment you had the first time, or you can blend them for a real taste sensation.

If you are running out of ingredients for an important recipe, you may want to go back to your leftover bin and scavenge for previous dishes that fit the bill.

- You may also find that leftovers can serve as filler. If you need to add more bulk to a casserole, mix in some leftovers.
- Try not to mix main-course leftovers with dessert leftovers. Such combinations are problematic.

B. Losing Weight

HACKER CUISINE IS ideal for weight loss. Although each dish may pack a whopping three to six thousand calories in itself, you will find that it is easy to lose weight using the regimen described here: the Hacker Weight-Loss Diet.

Dieting is as much a psychological game as it is an eating program. There are only two ways to lose weight through diet: you must either starve yourself physically (that is, refuse to eat anything) or starve yourself psychologically by refusing to eat anything that is good. Many people can fool themselves for a short time into thinking that they like sucking down celery shakes and salads and that they can eat small quantities of wonderful stuff. But they don't, and they can't—at least not for any length of time. Your body may stick to a starvation program while you are vigilant, but in a weak moment, resulting from such starvation itself, you will find yourself helplessly spooning hot fudge into your mouth.

The Hacker Weight-Loss Diet doesn't waste time *avoiding* this rather nifty paradigm. It *uses* it:
- During the day, eat absolutely nothing.
- At night, pig out.
- Throughout the day, continually hack.

There are no holds barred—everything is done to extreme. During the day, do not touch a thimbleful of food, not even a stick of celery! Then at night, eat anything and everything you can get your hands on for dinner. The only restriction is that you eat only one large gluttonous meal. Hacker cuisine is ideal because it is a complete overload of everything that you could possibly want.

With this diet, you are accomplishing three very basic goals. First, you have all the satisfaction of eating at night. Your subconscious no longer

works against you because you have made an implicit contract with it: You get whatever you want, so you are winning the psychological game. You'll find this to be an incredible relief.

By continuing to hack, you will lose all sense of time and with it your appetite. Your fixation on food will merge—at least momentarily—into your craft. Your mind will simply not think about food. Days will speed by (as they normally do in hacking). When you surface, you know that you can eat anything (as long as it is part of one long gluttonous dinner).

Finally, by fasting during the day, you lower your caloric intake and actually reduce your body's ability to consume large amounts of food. Your stomach will naturally shrink, and your feasts will naturally become rather small and unimpressive, at least in the world of hackers. It is a pathetic sight! For dieters, however, the shame of eating small quantities of hacker cuisine is offset by the knowledge that they are slimming down.

You can do this for years. Because roller coasting is simply the easiest way to diet, it is incorporated into the Hacker Weight-Loss Diet. When combined with hacking, it enables you to lose pounds while your hacking contributes in some way to society and technological advancement. It is a win-win-lose situation for everybody.

C. The Economics of Hacker Cuisine

LET'S DISPENSE WITH the myth that hacker food is intrinsically more expensive than traditional food. Although prepared food is priced higher than raw ingredients, common sense and a degree in economics reveal quite a different story. Traditional food preparation relies on slave labor: yours! If you are spending more time preparing the food than enjoying it, you are losing money.

The economy of hacker cuisine has been a source of pride for many years. The food is inexpensive, a true time saver, and fun to boot. This appendix takes an in-depth look at the economics of hacker cuisine and how it can improve your pocketbook.

The Dollar Value of Time

The first consideration is the value of your time. To find out the dollar value of your time, use the following steps:

1. Calculate the base value of your time by calculating your *effective hourly rate*. To do this, take your annual salary and divide by 2,080 hours, the number of work hours in a year. Do not factor in any dividends or interest you earn. Do not subtract taxes, the cost of benefits, and so on. If you

are working at a couple of jobs or do outside consulting, factor this in using weighted averaging. [2]

For each job, multiply the number of hours worked by the total revenue from that job. If you only have one job, your rate is simply the total earned income divided by the total number of hours that you worked.

For example, if you make $40,000 a year and bring in an additional $3,000 for sixty hours of outside work, then your effective rate is $20.09 an hour.

2. If you function as a housewife, the services you provide to your household should be factored in and averaged on an hourly basis. How much will it cost to replace your services with those of one or more outside helpers? To calculate your effective rate, use the basic approach of cost replacement.

Jobs	Rate on the outside	Number of hours/week	Rate x hours
Chauffeuring	$30/hr	14	$420
Child care	$10/hr	28	$280
Cleaning	$20/hr	16	$320
Cooking	$20/hr	21	$420
Counseling	$100/hr	4	$400
Escort services	$150/hr	8	$1,200
Gardening	$20/hr	8	$160
Paying bills	$20/hr	4	$80
Total		103	$3,280

[2] The basic formula is: $Rate_{hourly} = \dfrac{\sum_{i=jobs} (Dollars_i \times Hours_i)}{Total\ Hours}$

Take the total costs in the "Rate x hours" column and divide by total in the "Number of hours/week" column. For the example just given, the effective rate is $31.84 per hour.

On the whole, housewives have a much higher effective rate because their workweeks are longer and they provide some rather specialized services.

From these simple calculations, you can establish your effective hourly rate. On average, these rates will range from $12 to $50 per hour for salaried workers and $14 to $34 per hour for non-salaried live-in partners.

From these rates alone, it should be quite obvious that a traditional meal will cost more to prepare than a more enjoyable hacker meal. For example, a traditional meatloaf and mashed potato meal that takes one and a half hours to prepare will cost $28.85 for an average $40,000-a-year professional. Compare this to a plate of Oinkers that takes only ten minutes to fix at a cost of $3.21 for the same professional's time. That's an effective savings of $25.64. And the hacker meal will probably turn out better every time.

Equipment Depreciation

The time savings of hacker cuisine are not the only area with demonstrable cost savings: Hacker cuisine also requires less equipment than conventional cooking.

To calculate the overhead associated with the

appliances that you now have, use the following steps:

1. Make a list of all of your appliances and their costs.
2. Determine how many meals you normally prepare with each appliance per year.
3. Divide the cost of the appliance by the average number of meals you will use it for over its lifetime to arrive at the cost per meal of the appliance. Use a typical five-year depreciation schedule for your major appliances and a three-year depreciation schedule for your minor appliances.

The following table shows a calculation for an average kitchen. Notice that by simply storing the ingredients in the refrigerator and warming them up on the stove, you could be adding another $1 to the costs of preparing the meal, excluding any gas, electricity, or water that you may use.

AMORTIZATION OF CONVENTIONAL EQUIPMENT

Appliance	Cost	Life (yrs.)	Meals/yr.	Cost/meal
Oven	$800	5	50	$3.20
Cooktop	$600	5	150	$0.80
Refrigerator	$800	5	600	$0.27
Microwave	$500	5	400	$0.25
Pots/pans	$750	5	200	$0.75
Blender	$250	5	100	$0.50
Coffee maker	$100	3	300	$0.11
Coffee grinder	$100	3	300	$0.11
Toaster	$80	3	100	$0.27
Total				$6.26

AMORTIZATION OF HACKER EQUIPMENT

Appliance	Cost	Life (yrs.)	Meals/yr.	Cost/meal
Spoon	$3.50	5	1,095	$0.00
Bowl	$7.00	5	1,095	$0.00
Can Opener	$20.00	3	1,095	$0.01
Microwave	$200.00	3	450	$0.15
TOTAL				$0.16

Other Savings

You may also find hackers shopping at local convenience stores ten minutes before serving dinner. This is a natural, and in fact, desired behavior. After all, the meal is not going to take that long. Whereas your typical grocery store is quite large, requiring comfortable shoes and a road map to navigate, the convenience store is small, affording a comprehensive view of everything upon entry. Whereas the grocery store has a line at the express lane, the convenience store does not. The average number of items per customer is low. Because most convenience store clerks do not speak English—at least not well—there will be less idle, time-consuming chatter.

All of this translates to much quicker shopping trips which more than compensates for the higher prices. In general, shopping at convenience stores has become much more enjoyable these days. There are self-serve soda machines, coffee, nachos, popcorn, and hot dogs all within a stone's throw from any part of the store. Many a hacker has seized the opportunity to have dinner at such a store instead of shop for it. Where the convenience store encourages this behavior, it is frowned upon at your typical megagrocery, where the days of free samples and friendly service seem to be history. What a shame! Shopping can be a wonderful, sensory experience, but with the emphasis on lower prices, these stores are now interested in higher volumes. It is easy to project not far into the future that these stores might enforce ten-item minimums on all shoppers simply to cover overhead costs.

It is also true that hackers consume far more than your average mortal, contributing to a higher grocery bill, but luckily, the quantity and cost remain well under the amounts required by designer goods. For example, a pint of generic pork and beans checks out at $4 these days, whereas a pint of designer pork and beans can go for much more. This cost difference becomes ever clearer in the domain of spices: A normal recipe may call for saffron, at $12 per 1/32 of a gram, while hackers usually want only salt and pepper, available in ten-year supplies at an equivalent cost of $3.12.

Finally, with fewer pots and pans thrown into the mix, cleanup time is dramatically reduced. This becomes especially apparent when entertaining. Whereas a meal prepared in the traditional fashion may clutter the kitchen and adjoining rooms, the hacker has paced himself throughout the meal and may find cleanup limited to his arsenal of equipment: a bowl, a spoon, and perhaps the gummy mixture in the microwave. All of this takes but a few minutes to rectify and is hardly worth stopping the fun to do.

Buying in Bulk

With the advent of food clubs and warehouses, buying food in bulk has never been easier. It is recommended that all staples—Cheese Whiz, Spam, mayonnaise, soy sauce, bean dip, pretzels, chips, Coke—be purchased in large survival sizes suitable for fallout shelters. Although storage of these commodities may be at a premium in your apartment, the savings will more than justify the inconvenience of sleeping with cans. Some helpful hints:

- Pull out all shelves in your refrigerator and freezer, including the glass drawers meant for fresh vegetables. You will have little use for these. Instead, with widest widths on the bottom, stack your containers, four to six cans high.
- Don't bother to pull plastic wrap over the tops of opened cans: the bottom of the next can will act to seal the leftovers.
- Store containers in the same way in your closet or under your bed. Midnight snacks will be all that much closer, plus you will feel like you are sleeping in a food locker.

In short, the hacker life-style is inexpensive. Except for the uncontrollable urges to buy any new technology that hits the stores, food and its preparation hardly take a bite out of the hacker paycheck.

Putting It All Together

It becomes obvious when one compares two similar meals: Hacker cuisine offers a definite cost advantage. The big saving is, of course, time! This time translates directly into dollars. Where a conventional meal of lasagna and pie for five people costs about $86 to prepare, a similar meal of Pretzel Lasagna and Mashed Banana Cups will cost $25—a whopping 70 percent savings.

COMPARISON OF FOOD PREPARATION COSTS

	Traditional	Hacker
Time to shop	0.75 hour	0.15 hour
Time to prepare	1.5 hours	0.25 hour
Time to clean up	1 hour	0.2 hour
Cost of your time	$60.13	$12.95
Cost of equipment	$6.26	$0.16
Energy consumed	$0.03	$0.01
Ingredients	$19.60	$12.36
Total Costs	$86.02	$25.48
Savings		70%

Index